The Scene-by-Scene *Casablanca* Film Guidebook

A Detailed Look at the Hollywood Film Classic
MICHAEL WILLIAN

Copyright © 2019 by Michael Willian

All rights reserved.
Printed in the United States of America. No part of this publication may be reproduced, stored in a retrieval system or transmitted in any form or by any means without the author's prior written permission.

ISBN 978-0-9762429-1-8

Book design: Suzette Heiman

Cover and interior Casablanca film stills courtesy of Bison Archives and HollywoodHistoricPhotos.com. Remaining photos by Michael Willian.

Illustrations by Michael Willian. Café, airport and Paris street line drawing by Midwest IP LLC

Published by Kerpluggo Books

Visit michaelwillianbooks.com for more *Casablanca* film features and inside stories about my research for this guidebook.

For my parents

CONTENTS

INTRODUCTION vii

USING THIS GUIDE ix

FILM CHRONOLOGY x

WAR TIMELINE xii

THE ROAD TO CASABLANCA 1

EVERYBODY COMES TO RICK'S 33

THE GAME CONTINUES 65

WE'LL ALWAYS HAVE PARIS 87

THE BLACK MARKET 111

THE NIGHT IN CASABLANCA HEATS UP 125

THE PLANE TO LISBON 153

FILM MUSIC 169

ABOUT THE AUTHOR 171

INTRODUCTION

"It needs drastic revisions...but could work." That was the opinion of a Warner Bros. screenwriter in December 1941 after he assessed the play *Everybody Comes to Rick's* for a prospective film adaptation. Never could he have imagined he was staring at the foundation of an American film classic, *Casablanca*.

The odds definitely were not in favor of the play's success. Its author was not established, and the play itself had never actually seen the stage. Yet it caught the attention of Warner Bros. executive Hal Wallis, and the studio shelled out $20,000 for the rights, a sizable amount at the time for an unproven commodity.

It's easy to understand how some at Warner Bros. might have been skeptical. The play is one rough read, and if it had ever made it to production in its original form it had all the makings of a Broadway bust. Still, the play did come with plenty of intriguing raw material and Warner Bros. now had a financial incentive to make it happen. They kicked things off with a fresh title and then tapped its top talent to begin reshaping the content. Ten months later they had a screen gem.

So what is the allure of *Casablanca*? As a romance it surprises. For all his amazing talent, Humphrey Bogart is not exactly modern-day swoon material. And the stream of anger and bitterness flowing from his Rick Blaine character can leave you wondering how his love interest, Ilsa Lund, remains attracted to him. Yet somehow the audience feels the emotional tug.

As we see it, the film works because it nails several key elements—a gripping premise, superb casting, smart dialogue, scenes rich with detail and a captivating setting. The formula draws us in. We want to know more about the characters and activities swirling through the city and Rick's Café Américain.

And as we took a closer look at *Casablanca* we discovered to our surprise and delight that there is indeed so much more to learn and see. The film is teeming with historical references and tie-ins that over the course of so many decades have lost their context. In this guidebook we bring these references back to life.

Scene after scene contains small details that cry out for explanation. For example, we were struck by how much foreign language peppers the film, both verbal and written. When translated these references provide key context and often times a dash of poignancy or humor. Again, we will clue you in to this hidden layer of communication.

We promise that by the time you're finished with this guidebook you will have a deeper appreciation for, and understanding of, this special film.

USING THIS GUIDE

Before diving in, we recommend checking out two chronologies we pulled together for you. The film chronology clarifies the sequence and timing of events and vignettes in *Casablanca*, which we find hard to keep straight given the fast pace of the film and the fact that so many scenes take place in Rick's Café Américain and on consecutive nights. The World War II chronology provides background on wartime events leading up to the film's setting.

We have organized the film into chapters based on logical groupings of scenes. Each chapter begins with an overview of the scenes covered. Each scene overview is followed by topics relating to events occurring in the chapter, organized sequentially, under one of these headings: Closer Looks, Did You Know?, History Lesson, Just Wondering, Film Anecdotes, Cast Anecdotes, Music Notes, Random Thoughts and Explanation Required.

The guidebook makes for a great read all by itself. We provide plenty of context for each topic so you'll have no trouble understanding what we're talking about. We recommend reading it first to keep the flow going, then circling back to watch the film while using the guidebook as a companion. Of course, if you want instant gratification just keep the film handy and use the film video bookmarks we provide to help you pinpoint items of interest. (Keep in mind that versions can vary by a few seconds, so you may need to adjust for this.)

You will definitely want to examine, early and often, the illustrations we created for Rick's Café, the Casablanca Airport and Rick's Paris flashback. These took quite a bit of time to pull together, but it was well worth the effort as they add a whole new level of insight into the film. The illustrations for the nights at the Café are particularly handy as it's nearly impossible to figure out on the fly where scenes take place within the Café. Each illustration has a numbered index that enables you to see where key scenes occur in relation to one another.

Finally, in addition to the Music Notes that appear throughout the guidebook, we've also included a list of songs from the film.

FILM CHRONOLOGY

The city of Casablanca has a way of taking hold of its guests and not letting go. But our stay here will be brief. Excluding Rick and Ilsa's dalliance in Paris, the film covers a mere three days. Most of our time is spent mingling, carousing and eavesdropping in the shadowy confines of Rick's Café. The rest is divided mostly between Casablanca's black market, police headquarters, a cross-town bar called the Blue Parrot and, of course, the Casablanca Airport.

The film should not be too hard follow given its brief time span. It's just that with so many memorable vignettes appearing in rapid succession—particularly in the Café—keeping straight the exact sequence of events is a bit of a challenge. So we've thrown together a snappy chronology that lets you see when scenes take place in relation to one another. Give it a quick peruse and you'll be ready to investigate mysterious Casablanca.

DAY ONE—DECEMBER 2, 1941: Our first day in Casablanca starts in an open-air market with the local authorities rounding up suspects for the murder of two German couriers, and ends at the Café in the wee hours with Ilsa calling on a bitter, drunk and emotionally troubled Rick. In between, the following events take place:

- Major Strasser and his Nazi entourage arrive at the Casablanca Airport
- Ugarte asks Rick to temporarily safeguard two letters of transit lifted off the murdered German couriers
- Ferrari and Rick discuss business
- Captain Renault and Rick talk on the Café terrace, then repair to Rick's office where they discuss Victor Laszlo's arrival in Casablanca
- Ugarte is arrested as a suspect in the German courier murders
- Rick is questioned by Major Strasser
- Victor and Ilsa arrive at the Café, then connect with fellow Resistance member Berger
- Rick stumbles upon Ilsa as Sam plays "As Time Goes By" for her
- Major Strasser confronts Victor and Ilsa
- Rick and Ilsa reacquaint while in the company of Captain Renault and Victor

- Rick sulks in the Café after hours over Ilsa's unexpected appearance, recalling their heady days in Paris before receiving a late-night visitor

PARIS FLASHBACK—SPRING 1940-JUNE 11, 1940: In flashback mode, Rick takes us through his time with Ilsa in Paris. A springtime montage includes a boat ride on the River Seine, a drive though the city and countryside, afternoon drinks, a night on the town and some late-night romance. June 11 opens at a Paris café, with Rick and Ilsa learning that the Germans are nearing Paris. The action then moves to a nearby bistro, with Rick, Ilsa and Sam preparing to leave Paris. The day's final scene takes place at a Paris train station.

DAY TWO—DECEMBER 3, 1941: Our second day in Casablanca begins at 10:00 a.m. at Casablanca's police headquarters. In Captain Renault's office, Victor, Ilsa, Major Strasser and Captain Renault discuss Victor and Ilsa's future in Casablanca. The rest of the day is chock-a-block with activity:

- Rick pays a morning visit to Ferrari at the Blue Parrot
- Rick and Ilsa cross paths in the market, just outside the Blue Parrot
- Victor and Ilsa call on Ferrari in search of exit visas
- Tempers flare at the Café bar over Yvonne's socializing with the enemy
- Rick helps a Bulgarian couple gamble their way out of Casablanca
- Rick and Victor meet in Rick's office to discuss the letters of transit
- German and French Café patrons square off through song, prompting Major Strasser to close the Café
- Victor and Ilsa have a heart-to-heart talk in their hotel room
- Ilsa returns to the Café to confront Rick
- Victor seeks refuge from the authorities inside the Café before being arrested

DAY THREE—DECEMBER 4, 1941: Our third and final day in Casablanca also starts in Captain Renault's office, this time with Rick calling on Captain Renault to propose a mutually beneficial deal involving Victor and the letters of transit. Later in the day, Rick visits the Blue Parrot to finalize the sale of the Café to Ferrari. That evening, Rick is back at the Café for an encounter involving Ilsa, Victor, and eventually Captain Renault. Finally, all four head to the Casablanca Airport for the climatic unfoldings on the tarmac.

WAR TIMELINE

The film is loaded with references to actual wartime events. To help you see how these events fit into the World War II mosaic, we've included a war timeline covering some of Germany's 1938 pre-war aggressions through December 1941, which is the month in which *Casablanca* is set. We've also included in italics a few related film references.

1938

MARCH 12—Germany invades Austria; known as the Anschluss.

SEPTEMBER 30—Munich Pact signed by Germany, France, Great Britain and Italy, authorizing Germany to cede Czechoslovakia's northern Sudetenland region in October.

1939

MARCH 15—Germany invades Czechoslovakia. (*Czechoslovakia is Victor Laszlo's country.*)

SEPTEMBER 1—Germany invades Poland, marking the beginning of the war.

SEPTEMBER 3—Great Britain and France declare war on Germany.

SEPTEMBER 5—United States declares its neutrality in the war; also neutral are Portugal, Spain, Belgium, Norway and Sweden.

1940

APRIL 9—Germany invades Denmark and Norway. (*Norway is Ilsa Lund's country.*)

MAY 10—Germany invades Belgium, the Netherlands and Luxembourg.

MAY 12—Germany invades France.

MAY 15—The Netherlands surrenders to Germany.

MAY 26—Allied troops begin to evacuate mainland Europe at Dunkirk, France, after being encircled by the Germans.

MAY 28—Belgium surrenders to Germany.

JUNE 10—Italy declares war on France.

JUNE 11—*Last day of Rick's Paris flashback.*

JUNE 13—Paris declared an open city.

JUNE 14—German forces enter Paris.

JUNE 16—Philippe Pétain becomes head of France's government.

JUNE 22—Pétain's Vichy government signs armistice with Germany, dividing France into occupied and unoccupied zones.

JUNE 23—Hitler tours conquered Paris.

JULY 10—Germany begins air attacks on Great Britain; marks the beginning of the Battle of Britain.

SEPTEMBER—Great Britain withstands massive German bombing raids in the Battle of Britain.

SEPTEMBER 27—Germany, Italy and Japan sign Tripartite Pact.

OCTOBER 28—Italy invades Greece.

1941

MARCH 1—Bulgaria joins Axis powers. (*Bulgaria is the country of the refugee couple, Jan and Annina Brandel, who appear throughout the film.*)

APRIL 6—Germany invades Greece and Yugoslavia.

MAY—Germany ceases bombing raids on Great Britain.

JUNE 22—Germany invades Russia.

DECEMBER 2–4—*Dates on which Casablanca is set.*

DECEMBER 7—Japan attacks the United States at Pearl Harbor; the United States declares war on Japan.

DECEMBER 11—Germany and Italy declare war on the United States.

CHAPTER 1

THE ROAD TO CASABLANCA

"Realizing the importance of the case, my men are rounding up twice the usual number of suspects."
— Captain Renault

Our journey into the wilds of Casablanca, Morocco, begins with some much-needed background on why we're here in the first place. It's early December 1941, and that means there's a war on, folks, though America hasn't officially entered the fray yet. With help from a few visual aids, and some sobering war footage, we learn how matters have evolved since World War II kicked off in September 1939 with Germany's invasion of Poland. And so far it's looking pretty grim for the good guys.

First, a world globe reveals that the Axis powers—mainly Germany, Italy and Japan—are winning this real-life game of Risk. Indeed, an alarmingly large number of countries are shaded in their favor. One consequence of these drastic shifts in territorial control is that millions of Europeans are now refugees, trying desperately to outrun the German military juggernaut.

And there aren't many countries that fit the bill as safe havens for these refugees. America is an obvious choice, but getting there from Europe is no small trick. In fact, a narrator informs us that the only viable embarkation point from Europe to America is Lisbon, Portugal. Now on paper getting to Lisbon from, say, France doesn't seem too difficult—just a quick jaunt through Spain and you're there. But for reasons we'll discuss shortly it wasn't that easy.

A handy map details a circuitous refugee "trail" to Lisbon that has sprung up. Refugees first must hoof it down to southern France and the Mediterranean coastal city of Marseille, then catch a boat across the Mediterranean Sea to Algeria in North Africa, and then hop a train to Casablanca, Morocco. Once in Casablanca they have to make their way back north, either by plane or boat, to Europe and Lisbon.

And making it from Casablanca to Lisbon is no cinch. An "exit visa," you see, is required to gain passage out of the French protectorate of Morocco, and rest assured these visas come at a price. In fact, more than a few folks have found themselves stranded in Casablanca, searching in vain for that all-elusive ticket to freedom.

With this backdrop, we're now ready for a crash course on how things operate in wartime Casablanca. Through an all-points police bulletin we learn that two German couriers have been murdered on their way to Casablanca. Two letters of transit have been stolen from the couriers, golden tickets of sorts that would afford their possessors unrestricted passage out of Casablanca.

Given Germany's recent triumph over France it's no surprise that the Germans carry some weight in Casablanca, and they want the murderer caught, and fast. To appease them, Casablancan authorities descend on a market where merchants hustle their wares amid a throng of locals and transplants. Without notice the police start rounding up suspects. Most are taken to the station without incident, but when one tries to bolt he pays for the transgression with his life. Such is life, and death, on the hard-scrabble streets of Casablanca.

As market-goers recover from this disturbing but all-too-familiar episode, a plane flies overhead, steadying itself for landing at the nearby airport. On board are several officers of the Third Reich, the highest ranking of which is the villainous Major Strasser. Strasser is greeted on the tarmac with great ceremony by Captain Renault, Casablanca's Prefect of Police. At once, Strasser expresses his extreme displeasure over the recent murders. Renault, always quick on the uptake, assures him that all necessary steps are being taken to ensure that the murderer is caught. In fact, not only does Renault know who the murderer is, he knows where he can be found *that very night*. In Casablanca, you see, *everybody*—including murderers—comes to Rick's.

Opening Credits and Prologue

CLOSER LOOK: Our first order of business is to take a hard look at the map of Africa underlying the opening credits. We love this rendering for its vintage look. There are too many anomalies to allow us to pin down the precise time it depicts, most likely because the prop team used multiple maps as references. Most clues point to somewhere between 1920 (the year Tanganyika Territory began going by that name) and 1934 (the year the Sarra Triangle became part of Libya). But there are still parts that have us puzzled, such as, no borders showing Italian Somaliland and, instead of Gold Coast, a throwback reference to Ashanti.

In any event, here's a list of African lands the map references by name:

Algeria	Ethiopia	Nigeria
Anglo-Egyptian Sudan	French Equatorial Africa	Northern Rhodesia
Angola	French West Africa	Rio de Oro
Ashanti	Kenya	South West Africa
Bechuanaland	Libya	Tanganyika Territory
Belgian Congo	Madagascar	Tunisia
Cameroons	Morocco	Uganda
Egypt	Mozambique	Union of South Africa

While many of these names are still in play, in Africa's ever-shifting geopolitical landscape several have gone by the wayside. Picking a few, Bechuanaland is now Botswana, South West Africa is modern-day Namibia and Tanganyika Territory morphed into Tanzania.

CLOSER LOOK: We scarcely make it through the opening credits before getting our first of several crash courses on World War II history, courtesy of a handy world globe. The film's black and white format makes it tough to decipher the globe's color scheme, but with a few exceptions the dark-shaded countries are controlled by the Axis powers.

France is shown divided into two parts: northern France (including Paris and the entire Atlantic coastal region) and southern France. When the Germans won the Battle of France in June 1940, the armistice agreement France was forced to sign divided France into these two zones.

The northern zone remained under German military occupation, and thus became known as "occupied France." The Germans elected not to occupy the southern zone (including France's holdings in Africa); hence the zone was dubbed "unoccupied France." (Captain Renault and others use this term throughout the film.) Post-armistice, the Germans allowed a new French government—known as "Vichy"—to oversee unoccupied France, but of course in practice the Vichy government answered to the Third Reich.

HISTORY LESSON: In the first of many historical sidebars, let's take a quick look at how France, including its Moroccan protectorate, came to be under the thumb of the Germans. In May 1940, the Germans launched a two-act invasion, often referred to in whole as the Battle of France.

First, starting on May 10, 1940, Germany invaded the Low Countries—basically the Netherlands, Belgium and poor little Luxembourg, plus the northernmost part of France. The offensive included a merciless bombing of Rotterdam, and a land romp west to the Atlantic Ocean. The rugged Ardennes forest was supposed to protect the Low Countries from such a land advance, but Germany's armored panzer divisions *blitzkrieged* their way through it in just three weeks.

In the first days of June, the Germans turned their attention to the rest of France. Two German army groups, comprised of some six dozen army divisions, plunged south with Paris in their sights. By June 9 one group seized Rouen, eighty miles northwest of Paris. Days later the other group took Reims, less than a hundred miles northeast of Paris. At this point, Paris was starting to look a touch vulnerable.

So how did things go from there? We'll save that part of the story for Rick and Ilsa's Paris flashback.

RANDOM THOUGHTS: The globe is a serviceable enough reference but, with apologies to the film's special effects team, it has the look and feel of an eighth-grade science project. The only thing missing is an erupting volcano. The swirling clouds around Antarctica are a nice enough touch, but if a dash of realism was the aim, the team would have done well to go without the place names.

CLOSER LOOK: The globe's depiction of country borders is quite rough, and perhaps the most glaring distortion involves Morocco—the one country that you'd think would have received special attention. The easternmost border of Morocco is, in fact, directly south of Spain. But on this globe, Morocco extends hundreds of miles east of Spain. **(1:30)** In effect, the globe's designer ceded to Morocco the entire coastal region of Algeria. In fairness, this was likely done on purpose to make the featured country more visible.

EXPLANATION REQUIRED: Look also for a prominent mountain range in the middle of Germany. Yes, Germany's central uplands are hilly and feature some modestly mountainous terrain, but it doesn't look anything like what's shown here, either in scale or profile. Now, this may well simply be another inadvertent cartographic miss. Or, more interestingly, it's possible the special effects team was having some fun here—to our eye the configuration looks like a loose interpretation of the Third Reich's infamous swastika.

CAST ANECDOTES: The main benefit of using a film narrator is setting a scene on the quick, leaving more time for the stuff that matters. In *Casablanca*, the film's premise is smartly established in just over a minute by a narrator who tells us why everyone is attracted to Casablanca like moths to a flame.

The voice of the narrator is Lou Marcelle, a sometime radio actor and announcer who landed film "appearances" now and then as the faceless narrator. A few months after *Casablanca* wrapped, Warner Bros. tapped Marcelle to set up *Background to Danger* in similar fashion, complete with maps and a globe. While this wartime espionage romp misses the mark with dated dialogue and a half-baked plot, it does reunite *Casablanca* stars Sidney Greenstreet and Peter Lorre, and they are fun to watch playing Nazi and Russian agents at cross purposes. Later on, we'll clue you in to a fascinating connection that *Background to Danger* has to *Casablanca*.

So was Marcelle's undoing in film the fact that he had a face for radio? To judge for yourself, track down a 1946 romantic comedy starring Errol Flynn called *Never Say Goodbye,* in which Marcelle, donning a pencil-thin moustache, plays a radio announcer (naturally) and appears on screen for several seconds.

RANDOM THOUGHTS: Marcelle may have been a first-rate radioman but the pronunciation of one word seems to have eluded him here. Who knew that refugees in Casablanca were actually searching for exit *vhee-zaays*?

DID YOU KNOW?: If you're thinking that the route shown here for refugees making their way to Casablanca would be fun to retrace on your next vacation, you can pretty well forget it. The main problem is that, however inviting Algeria may have been in its days as a French protectorate, today it is one dangerous place to hang out. The country has been plagued by social and political unrest for decades, and violent extremist groups continue to pose a threat to foreigners, particularly in rural areas.

But even if you're game for crossing the Mediterranean Sea to Algeria and striking out from Oran, you actually can't go overland between Algeria and Morocco. Morocco closed the border in 1994 in response to a terrorist attack attributed to Algerian nationals. So unless you're comfortable with an illegal border crossing by camel we don't recommend this high adventure.

HISTORY LESSON: The montage shows several ships tramping across the Mediterranean Sea, creating the impression that refugees could shove off from Marseille, France, to North Africa any old time. In fact, finding a boat out of Marseille would have been a huge hurdle in any trek to Casablanca. At a minimum one needed an exit visa to leave France legally. Absent an exit visa, illegal boat passage was a high-risk proposition. The waters around Marseille were well patrolled and any boat found slinking in or around the harbor would be nabbed in no time, with all aboard virtually assured a trip to a French concentration camp.

DID YOU KNOW?: You probably suspected as much, but the French government never issued anything equivalent to the "letter of transit" described in the film. Still, the film did get the basics right. Not only were exit visas required in order to legally leave unoccupied France, but they were extraordinarily hard to come by.

HISTORY LESSON: The film accurately describes Lisbon, Portugal, as the destination of choice for anyone bent on fleeing Europe. This was true for several reasons. First and foremost, politically Portugal declared itself neutral in the war and had a history of general tolerance for war transients. Secondly, geographically Portugal was well insulated from the war, being at the tip of the Iberian Peninsula and surrounded by neutral Spain. Third, and more practically, throughout the war Lisbon enjoyed regular air and boat service from the Americas.

Still, the Marseille-Oran-Casablanca-Lisbon route touted in the film was by no means the route of choice. Indeed, that route presented plenty of risk since Algeria and Morocco both were governed by Vichy. And a refugee caught by the Vichy government in French North Africa without the requisite travel papers was more than likely headed for an extended stay in a Vichy-run labor camp in Algeria.

The far more logical and accessible route to Lisbon was through Spain. And while this route also came with risk at least you didn't have to deal with the Vichy government over and over again. Timing was everything if going through Spain. Just after the June 1940 armistice, Spain was unpredictable day-to-day on whether it would afford refugees passage through to Lisbon. But if you picked the right border crossing on the right day, you were on your way.

DID YOU KNOW?: Some daring male refugees did in fact make their way from France to Casablanca using the route shown in the film by posing as French soldiers. With the fall of Paris, tens of thousands of French soldiers received their military demobilization papers and were sent home. Soldiers returning to French Morocco would first be transported to Marseille, then ferried over to North Africa and then taken by train to Casablanca. Industrious refugees stuck in Marseille would bribe a sympathetic French officer for an authentic set of demobilization papers, pick up a uniform on the black market (no problem) and memorize just enough details of their supposed military days to withstand some basic questioning.

DID YOU KNOW?: So how could refugees get from France to Lisbon legitimately? Well, for starters a French exit visa was a must. But that was just one of many process hurdles. Let's say you wanted to go the traditional route, by land via Spain. Here are some of the details you needed to work through:

French Transit Papers. Also called "safe conduct papers," you would need these to travel to the France-Spain border.

Foreign Entry Visa. To leave France or obtain a transit visa from Portugal, you needed proof that another country had agreed to take you. (Remember, Portugal was not a final destination, but rather an embarkation point for some other country.) U.S. visas were the most coveted, but they were exceedingly hard to come by. So other more obscure countries came into play: Brazil, Cuba, Congo, China, Haiti, Siam, Mexico, you name it. And if you used a forged entry visa to get to Lisbon, once you got there the heat was on to secure a legitimate one before the Portuguese authorities got wise and deported you.

Transit Visas for Spain and Portugal. Reaching your country of final destination required you to travel through Spain and Portugal, and you needed a transit visa from both countries authorizing the one-time cross-country trek. Spain would not issue a transit visa unless you already had a Portuguese transit visa.

Valid Passport. At first blush having a valid passport may seem like the least of your worries, but if you were, say, a refugee who had been deprived of your nationality by Nazi order then you no longer had access to a legal passport. So your hope here was to obtain a forged one—a risky and pricy proposition.

The upshot here is that the odds of having all the requisite papers in hand and valid at the same time were slim to none; hence the burgeoning market for forged papers and border smugglings.

JUST WONDERING: Even if letters of transit did exist, would they really be one's path to freedom under the circumstances? They are stolen property, and two German couriers are dead. Knowing this, surely the Nazis, who have plenty of influence in French Morocco, would simply demand that French authorities detain anyone attempting to travel on such papers. For what it's worth, the film's writers, producer and director were aware of the flaw, but in the end invoked artistic license.

Casablanca's Black Market

DID YOU KNOW?: Our first view of Casablanca is of a tower looming above a town market. The tower is actually a *minaret*, a central mosque feature in Islamic architecture. Minarets are used to alert Muslims to their Islamic daily prayer times.

CLOSER LOOK: Indeed, look for a man standing on the balcony of the minaret. He is not a tourist taking in the view but, rather, a *muezzin* or "crier" whose job it is to tell Casablanca's Muslims that it's time to face Mecca and commence praying. Yet as the camera pans down to the market below, we see that the crowd has not yet responded to his call to prayer.

CLOSER LOOK: At the base of the minaret is another item of Islamic architectural interest—a pointed horseshoe arch that forms the entrance to the mosque. **(2:07)** While the Romans championed the arch and made widespread use of the traditional semicircular variant, Muslims are believed to have originated the pointed arch, and Muslim architects certainly mastered the form. Pointed arches are no doubt aesthetically pleasing and have the added bonus of actually being stronger than semicircular arches.

FILM ANECDOTES: While this scene has a few nods to local religious culture, the original script had many more. For example, the muezzin was originally to be heard praying, with chants of "Allah, Allah, Allah." Later, after being gunned down, the murder suspect was supposed to chant the Islamic saying, "No god but Allah." The clear message being conveyed to moviegoers: things are different in Morocco.

But producer Hal Wallis found the religious references to be distracting and urged director Michael Curtiz to drop most of them, including the muezzin's lines, which Wallis referred to as "the Allah, Allah business." Wallis also nixed some accompanying Moroccan-style music after concluding that the whole thing had the feel of an "operetta." In the end, only the shot of the muezzin standing atop the minaret survived Wallis' artistic pullback.

CLOSER LOOK: On the left side of the street is a shop called *La Bonne Odeur*, or The Good Smell, which boasts, in French, that it sells "brand-name perfumes" and "glassworks from the country." In the street keep an eye out for a man juggling, another selling bread (hanging from a pole), two kids throwing a ball into a basket, two men haggling over the price of two monkeys, a donkey lugging its load through the crowd, a man selling Moroccan candy (halawat) from a pole and a couple of parrots perched atop another pole. Just a typical day in Casablanca's black market.

FILM ANECDOTES: Production materials disclose that the tight-fisted Warner Bros. saved several thousand dollars in production expenses by reusing sets built for the Warner Bros. films *The Desert Song* and *Now, Voyager*, both of which were in production at the same time as *Casablanca*. We wondered just how similar the *Casablanca* versions of these borrowed sets were to the ones used in those films, and this scene offers the first opportunity to compare sets.

Recycling sets from *The Desert Song* was an easy call since it too was set in Morocco, and the production team had already spent considerable time and money creating the appropriate local atmosphere. It took some doing to track down a copy of *The Desert Song*—Warner Bros. basically mothballed the film due to copyright issues—but what we discovered was a shot nearly identical to the one here. The perspective, looking up a narrow winding street, is the same. The arch's bricking and timber supports are the same, as are the storefront awnings lining the street. And the scene created in *The Desert Song* is the same cacophonic swirl of merchants, hustlers, buyers and animals, only with a slightly more authentic feel. Interestingly, in *The Desert Song* you get a view not afforded in *Casablanca*—a shot from the top of the street looking down.

Beyond *Casablanca*'s black market set, look for the façade of the Palais de Justice (identifiable by the balcony) and yes, Rick's Café. There's no mistaking that the café run by Père Fan-Fan in *The Desert Song* is a reconfigured Rick's. It's smaller than Rick's, with more of a Blue Parrot vibe, but it's hard to miss the structural similarities. The stairs in Rick's are reworked to tie into Pere Fan Fan's main entrance. Rick's balcony overlooking the café, and the underpass to the gambling room are virtually unchanged. The bar is in the same place. Overall, you don't really even need to squint your eyes to see Rick's. These café scenes alone make tracking down *The Desert Song* well worth the effort.

As for the set borrowed from *Now, Voyager*, it surfaces in the last scene of the Paris flashback. We'll discuss that set when the time comes.

RANDOM THOUGHTS: *Casablanca* and *The Desert Song* are both set in Morocco, but Warner Bros. did a better job in *The Desert Song* creating an exotic, faraway-land atmosphere. One key difference is the score. *The Desert Song* is filled with plausibly native music whereas *Casablanca* relies on traditional, orchestrated material. Another is the film's use of extended scenes shot on location in the Arizona desert, complete with Moroccan warriors battling on horseback. These scenes make the film feel far less confined than *Casablanca*, which is essentially a studio back-lot affair.

FILM ANECDOTES: More than a few film mavens believe that a 1937 French film called *Pépé-le-Moko* had a strong influence on *Casablanca*. The film is about a gruff but engaging Parisian jewel thief (Pépé) who is on the lam and has managed to elude the authorities by hiding out in the Casbah, the infamous devils-den section of the Algiers, Algeria. When a beautiful Parisian girl (Hedy Lamarr) visits the Casbah, Pépé falls for her and as a result becomes susceptible to being lured out of the Casbah's safe environs.

Well, we screened *Pépé-le-Moko* as well as the nearly identical Hollywood remake of it, *Algiers* (1938). Indeed, there are some common threads—the brash personas of Pépé and Rick Blaine, the basic parable of love and love lost, and Pépé and Rick's cat-and-mouse friendship with a local official—though nothing that would have casual moviegoers making an immediate connection. That said, we were pleasantly surprised to see that in both versions the role of the police informant is played by a *Casablanca* actor: Marcel Dalio in *Pépé-le-Moko* and Lionid Kinskey in *Algiers*.

Police Communications Room

DID YOU KNOW?: Sandwiched in between black market scenes is one of a local official broadcasting an all-points bulletin to be on the lookout for suspects in the murder of two German couriers. The official rips the bulletin off of what's known as a teletype machine, which were state of the art back then for remote communications, and, practically speaking, performed rather like large automated typewriters.

CLOSER LOOK: Behind the local official is a large wall map. Give it a quick look and see if you can spot it later in the film, only in an entirely different setting.

JUST WONDERING: Why does the bulletin declare at the end, rather than the beginning, that the broadcast is "Important"?

The Black Market

CLOSER LOOK: A police car (*Police Municipale Marocaine* is on the side door) is shown zooming through the market in pursuit of suspects. **(2:46)** Three separate clips of the car appear in rapid succession, creating the impression that the officers are covering some serious ground. But closer scrutiny reveals that the car actually passes the same stretch of market stall fronts all three times. We know this because in all three clips the car passes the same poster hanging on a market wall. Oops. So mark down a film gaffe for overuse of a film set.

DID YOU KNOW?: On the radiator grille of the police car you can see the famous Mercedes-Benz tri-pointed star logo. And in slow motion you can see tri-points on the wheel covers. **(2:47)** Now, whether a city in a French protectorate would have a fleet of high-end German-made police cars is a matter for debate. But a Mercedes-Benz definitely was the ride of choice for Hitler and his Third Reich cronies, so using one here would be appropriate at least on that stretched level.

CLOSER LOOK: Identifying the model of this car should have been easy. Oddly, though, we could not match it with any car made by Daimler-Benz or its predecessors. In the end we discovered that this is not a Mercedes-Benz at all, but rather a 1927 Lincoln L Series sport touring car disguised as a Mercedes-Benz to better fit in with the film's foreign setting.

The car's grille has been swapped out and mock wheel covers have been installed to give it foreign plausibility. Other than that, it's pure Lincoln. This was a high-end car in its day, ideal for open-air road excursions. It's a seven-seater, with two fold out jump seats located in the cavernous back compartment, just in front of the back seats. In the airport scene at the end of the film, as the car drives onto the tarmac, you can see two rows of passengers in the back. Lastly, we think the same car appears in another Warner Bros. film, *Background to Danger*, released just a few months after *Casablanca*.

CLOSER LOOK: The officer who blows his whistle shouts in French, "Go, Boy!"—your standard French phrase for "Clear the way." And market-goers would be wise to heed his order, what with a police car now barreling through the souk. Indeed, on its third pass the car sends several folks scrambling for safety. Two manage to avoid the car's left front fender, while another comes close to getting tagged by the right one. **(2:56)** Looks to us like one stuntman got more than he bargained for here.

JUST WONDERING: In Casablanca, does rounding up "all suspicious characters" mean detaining anyone wearing a coat and tie? Every man nabbed by the authorities is dressed pretty darn well for a suspected murderer.

EXPLANATION REQUIRED: At the police wagon, a policeman barks, in French, the following instructions to the suspects: "Go to the wagon. Go. Right now. Get in." The script identifies these policemen as *gendarmes*. French gendarmes skew more toward military than police in nature, and historically have patrolled France's rural regions. Gendarmes will play a role in several other key scenes, including Ugarte's arrest, the closing of Rick's Café, Victor Laszlo's arrest and Major Strasser's shooting.

RANDOM THOUGHTS: When a gendarme shouts at a fleeing suspect to halt, he does so in English, not French. Now having foreign characters speak in English is a long-standing Hollywood tradition. But this film sprinkles in a surprisingly large amount of foreign dialogue—French, German, Italian, even some Russian—so they might just as well have had the policeman say "Arret!" We would have gotten the gist.

DID YOU KNOW?: The official language of Morocco back then was Arabic, one language you won't hear in the film. (There are a few Arabic signs, which we will point out as they appear.) And since 2011 Morocco has a second official language, Tamazight, a native language of Morocco's Berber people. Still, anyone doing business in Morocco these days would do well to brush up on their French as it is a common choice for Moroccan commercial and governmental affairs.

CLOSER LOOK: As the prime suspect bolts, the camera follows him briefly before coming to rest on two bystanders, an attractive couple out for a market stroll. **(3:31)** Here, they are just faces in the crowd, but this is in fact the first of several scenes in which the couple appears. From the script we learn their names, Jan and Annina Brandel. Later on, Annina explains that they are refugees from Bulgaria and they are desperate to get to America. So much so that Annina considers taking unmentionable steps to obtain exit visas for them both.

Ah, but we are getting ahead of ourselves. For now, try to keep track of how many times Jan and Annina appear during the film. We'll give you the official tally when they make their last appearance.

CLOSER LOOK: Behind Jan and Annina hang sun hats that look suspiciously like sombreros. **(3:31)** Distant cousins, we suppose, of something called a taraza that you might find women wearing in Spanish-influenced towns in northern Morocco; but in Casablanca, not so much. Below the hats hangs a sign in Arabic that appears to be a prayer from the Koran.

RANDOM THOUGHTS: Check out the path that our not-so-fleet-footed suspect takes while trying to escape. He has so much trouble turning onto a side street that if the police hadn't shot him he'd have run straight into the wall. **(3:36)** Now, *that* would have been embarrassing.

CLOSER LOOK: Here we find the first in a series of scene continuity gaffes. Look for the woman dressed like a circus carny, leaning casually against the wall to the left of the poster. **(3:39)** No matter that a man has just been gunned down at her feet, she's one cool customer. But in the shot just before the suspect falls she can be seen standing with two others well away from the wall. Also, as the gendarmes gather the fallen suspect's papers you can see a table and a piece of pottery beneath the poster, but neither is visible in the previous shots. **(3:30)**

CLOSER LOOK: The gendarmes take down the suspect in front of a large poster that promotes Philippe Pétain, one of the more controversial characters in French history. At the time Pétain headed the aforementioned post-armistice Vichy France government.

The French-language poster translates to, "I hold my promises, even those from others. Philippe Pétain, Marshal of France." Pétain actually said something close to this in a March 1941 national radio address, and here's the back-story.

The winter of 1940-41 took its toll on the French citizenry. As if the German invasion and occupation weren't bad enough, the winter was unusually harsh, leading to severe food shortages. With the public's mood blackening and Pétain's popularity plummeting, Pétain was desperate to offer up some good news.

He did so by tackling the long and hotly debated domestic issue of retirement pensions. Previous French governments had promised pensions but none had delivered. Pétain saw this as an opportunity to create some goodwill, and announced that the Vichy government would be the one to finally keep the promise. The actual words spoken by Pétain translated to, "I hold the promises, same as those of others, when these promises are founded on justice."

RANDOM THOUGHTS: If Pétain looks a little long in the tooth in the poster, it's with good reason. He assumed leadership of the Vichy government in 1940 at the not-so-spry age of eighty-four.

HISTORY LESSON: So how did an octogenarian become head of the Vichy government? Mostly by being a war hero. During World War I, Pétain gained a reputation as an architect of victory. This was based mainly on his performance in the 1916 Battle of Verdun, which was widely viewed as the turning point of the war. Indeed, his defense of Verdun earned him the honorific nickname Victor at Verdun. Not long after the war he was elevated to the lofty French military status of marshal.

Now, knowing all of this, one would think that when France's next scuffle with the Germans came around, Pétain would have little trouble choosing sides. But things were not so clear to Pétain. Curiously, he also saw Britain as a natural enemy of France, and between the wars concluded that a French-German alliance was the preferred path to long-term peace in Europe.

In 1939, Pétain was serving as France's ambassador to Spain. In May 1940, with things looking bleak in the Battle of France, the Prime Minister of France asked Pétain to join his revamped war cabinet on the strength of Pétain's military experience and war hero status. By mid-June France was in a world of trouble. Germany controlled Paris and the French government was scrambling to regain its footing in a new capital. The prime minister abruptly resigned and Pétain took control of what became known as the Vichy government. Just days after assuming leadership Pétain entered into an armistice with the Nazis, adopting a strategy of collaboration and appeasement. Pétain had effectively committed the Vichy government to carrying out the Nazi government's unspeakable practices and he was never anything but Hitler's pawn.

DID YOU KNOW?: The Vichy government got its name from the southern France town of Vichy, which served as the new French government's capital. So how was Vichy bestowed the ignominious distinction of being the capital of unoccupied France? In early June 1940, with the Germans bearing down on the French capital of Paris, the French government beat a hasty retreat out of town, first to an area near Tours, and then, just a few days later, farther southwest to Bordeaux.

A few weeks later the armistice signed by Germany and France carved France into occupied and unoccupied zones. Germany, for the time being, allowed France to retain governmental control of the unoccupied zone. But Bordeaux ended up in the occupied zone, so it was out as the new capital.

After considering Clermont-Ferrand and Lyon, Pétain's band chose the mineral-spa resort town of Vichy, primarily for its central location and abundance of hotels, which translated into office space for the nomadic government. Pétain thereafter took every opportunity to convince Hitler to let the government move back to Paris, but Hitler was not interested in giving up the crown jewel of his conquests.

DID YOU KNOW?: This poster of Pétain would not have been the first time Casablancans had come across Pétain. Back in the 1920s, Spain and France sought to enhance their colonial control of Morocco, but Spain proved no match for local Berber opposition forces. In 1925, Pétain recognized the interest both countries had in defeating local forces, and hatched a plan with Spain's leader to join arms. A year later Pétain had, in effect, orchestrated Spain's retaking of Spanish Morocco. So it's understandable that some Moroccans would not be particularly thrilled about Pétain resurfacing.

EXPLANATION REQUIRED: Backing up a bit here, it turns out that the poster hanging in the market—the one we used to confirm that the police car had passed by the same spot three different times—also depicts Pétain. This French-language poster translates to, "I made a gift of myself to the fatherland." **(2:54)** Wow, this guy really knew how to pen the propaganda.

As with the previous Pétain poster, the quote used here can be traced to an actual Pétain speech. In a June 17, 1940, radio address, just three days after the Germans overtook Paris, Pétain announced to all of France that he was now the head of the French government. His actual words translated to, "I give to France the gift of my person to lessen her misfortune."

Heady stuff to be sure, but that same speech also included a notorious linguistic blunder. Pétain told the people that it was necessary for France to cease fighting. No problem there, but what he forgot to tell people was exactly *when* they were supposed to cease fighting. Half the military thought Pétain had called for an immediate surrender, while the other half thought they were obliged to fight until a formal cease-fire was announced. Two days and several hundred casualties later, the whole thing got straightened out when the Germans formally agreed to cease fighting pending the signing of an armistice.

HISTORY LESSON: As the murder suspect lies dying, we get a brief glimpse of some papers he's carrying. While this guy may not be the one who murdered the two German couriers, he's still trouble in the Vichy government's eyes. The papers confirm that he has an allegiance to Free France, which was the French government-in-exile formed by General Charles de Gaulle in the aftermath of the German occupation.

De Gaulle was taking the fight to the Germans as they rolled through the Low Countries and northern France in May 1940. But when things became bleak, his superiors called him off the battlefield and gave him diplomatic responsibility for brokering a joint plan with Great Britain that avoided an all-out French surrender. When the French government finally decided to cave to the Germans, de Gaulle headed for London and anointed himself the leader of what he called the Free France forces. In a radio speech for the ages, de Gaulle proclaimed that defeat was not at hand, and in her fight "France is not alone!" He then invited all able-bodied Frenchmen to join his London-based government-in-exile. Of course, the newly-formed Vichy government did not take too kindly to this. In absentia, they court-martialed de Gaulle and sentenced him to death.

Building the Free France forces was a formidable task, and de Gaulle understandably relied heavily on British backing. Two months after being formed, Free France had just a few thousand members. And a disastrous initial military endeavor—a failed invasion of Dakar, the coastal capital of French West Africa—didn't exactly help its credibility. Still, by November 1940 Free France had managed to rally all of the territories of French Equatorial Africa plus Cameroon. While these territories were fairly easy pickings, they did offer some strategic value, plus numbers matter when you're starting from scratch.

CLOSER LOOK: The Free France papers have several interesting features, one of which is the key to deciphering a covert exchange that takes place later in Rick's Café. The larger pamphlet reads "Help Free France" and has a logo with the letter "F" positioned back-to-back.

The smaller one is of all things a Free France postcard. Some crack research indicates that it's actually authentic. A Free France propaganda campaign using postcards? Any means to get the word out for the French Resistance, we suppose. Just remember that it's not for use in France, given its propensity to reveal both sender and recipient as enemies of Vichy!

Anyway, on the postcard are two items of intrigue—a Free France logo and a photo of what looks like a boat. The logo is a double-barred cross, with the top bar shorter than the bottom one, overlaid with the words *France Libre* (Free France). The cross is the Cross of Lorraine. In 1940, the Free France government-in-exile adopted this cross as its official emblem. This same cross was incorporated into the Free France flag—the French tricolor with the cross centered in red. **(3:47)** Remember what the cross looks like, because it explains why, just a few scenes from now, Victor Laszlo suddenly becomes so trusting of a man trying to sell him a ring.

As for the photo on the postcard, it's actually a French submarine called the *Surcouf*. At the time the *Surcouf* was the flagship of the Free France navy, which explains perfectly why it's featured on this piece of Free France propaganda. The back of this postcard (illegible in the film) accurately explains that the *Surcouf* was "the largest submarine in the world." So of course it would be the pride of the French fleet, particularly since the Free France navy was running a little thin on tonnage at the time. The photo shows the *Surcouf* at sail. The submarine's conning tower and gun turret are visible just to the right of the gendarme's thumb. Farther to the right a few dozen submariners are lined up on the ship's deck, keeping their ears perked no doubt for the dive alarm. **(3:47)**

HISTORY LESSON: The *Surcouf's* participation in World War II was short on time but long on intrigue and controversy. When Germany invaded France in June 1940, the *Surcouf* scurried across the English Channel seeking safer waters. The British, who were taking no chances as to the allegiances of French naval vessels, promptly seized the submarine. The British eventually handed the *Surcouf* back to the Free France forces, but over the next several months the British started to suspect that the submarine was taking orders from Vichy and actually targeting and sinking British ships.

Whatever the case, in December 1941 (the month in which *Casablanca* is set) Free France leaders ordered the *Surcouf* to head a flotilla to Saint Pierre and Miquelon, a French territorial off the coast of Newfoundland technically under Vichy governance. In no time the *Surcouf* liberated the islands from Vichy and claimed them for Free France.

Unfortunately, the end was near for the *Surcouf*. Just two months later the boat left Bermuda headed for the Panama Canal, but she never made it. Her sinking remains a mystery, with theories including a collision with a U.S. freighter and friendly fire from a U.S. Navy vessel.

RANDOM THOUGHTS: Two years after *Casablanca*, Warner Bros. released another wartime adventure, *Passage to Marseille* (1944). On paper it sure seemed like another angle on *Casablanca*, and the studio definitely pitched it as such in film trailers. The cast was loaded with actors from *Casablanca*—Bogart, Claude Rains, Sydney Greenstreet, Peter Lorre, Helmut Dantine, Charles La Torre (Captain Tonelli in *Casablanca*), even

Corinna Mura, who in both films delivers pleasing guitar-strumming numbers. And like *Casablanca*, the film focuses on the sacrifices of the Resistance fighters.

But that's where the similarities end. Bogart stars as a French reporter (thankfully he doesn't attempt an accent) who takes a stand against the fascist leanings of some of his countrymen. He pays for his stand with an extended overseas prison stay on French Guiana's infamous Devil's Island, but later leads a group of escapees (including Lorre and Dantine) back to Vichy-controlled Marseille to join the fight against the Germans.

Palais de Justice and Préfecture de Police

DID YOU KNOW?: A sign above the entrance to the Palais de Justice (a French courthouse) reads *Liberté, Égalité, Fraternité* or Freedom, Equality, Brotherhood. This democratic motto has its origins in the French Revolution. It was the official motto of the French Third Republic and remains France's official motto today. But when the Vichy government assumed power from the Third Republic, Pétain replaced the motto with Labor, Family, Fatherland, a conservative and paternalistic triad that aligned with Pétain's vision of a more rural, church-focused France.

CLOSER LOOK: Above the motto is a coat-of-arms consisting of three vertical colored bands with a five-point star (also known as the seal of Soloman) and crescent centered in the middle band. The star and crescent symbols certainly fit the situation—they are two prominent symbols of Islam, the principal religion of Morocco. But we haven't been able to trace this configuration to any coat-of-arms or flag associated with either Morocco or Casablanca.

Since 1915 the Moroccan flag has been red with a green five-pointed star in the middle. Given that the same star-and-crescent configuration appears on all the local police vehicles, it's clear the prop team intended the coat-of-arms to be local in nature. But no matter—it's not authentic.

CLOSER LOOK: A directory located to the right of the entrance explains the layout of the courthouse. **(3:54)** You can't see the entire directory in the film, but we've provided the English version of what's visible. In a nice attention to detail, the sign pretty well captures the names of various courts in the French court system.

GROUND FLOOR
Registrar Records
Bailiff
Small Claims Court
First Civil Law Court
FIRST FLOOR
Criminal Court
Serious Crimes Court
Chamber of [Illegible]
SECOND FLOOR
Appellate Court
[Illegible]
THIRD FLOOR
[Illegible]

CLOSER LOOK: Conveniently for us, Casablanca's resident pickpocket explains to an English couple what is happening across the street at the courthouse. After the murder of two German couriers, they are witnessing a customary roundup of suspects, which, in addition to refugees and liberals, inevitably ensnares a few pretty girls for Captain Renault's entertainment. We will soon learn that Renault very much likes the ladies. But take a close look at the women exiting the refugee roundup wagon—they aren't exactly pin-ups. **(4:18)**.

FILM ANECDOTES: So why no beautiful young girls exiting the wagon? Because this is one scene the film censors took a stance on. Originally the scene featured a beautiful blonde stepping off the wagon, just as the pickpocket explained that Renault's roundups usually include a pretty young girl or two. The pickpocket was then to add cheekily, "the refugees and liberals will be released in a few hours…the girl will be released in the morning." This is just one example of how the censors softened or eliminated references to Renault's taste for the ladies.

CLOSER LOOK: The English chap, who has just been relieved of his wallet by one of Casablanca's ubiquitous vultures, is sporting two accessories that haven't quite withstood the test of time: a monocle and a zebra-print tie.

CLOSER LOOK: Out in the streets, as market-goers spy a plane overhead, we spy a number of signs in French. **(4:56)** The sign above the building entrance tells us we are in front of the police station (*Préfecture de Police*), which presumably is just around the corner from the courthouse we saw in the last scene. The French traffic sign in the foreground reads No Parking; the one in the background reads No Entry.

On the left, beneath the overhang, is a poster for what is presumably a local theater, *Théâtre d'Art*. The featured performance is *Féerie du Nu*, which if the name holds true means folks will be seeing a fairytale-like play performed with a bit of nudity thrown in. Near the bottom the poster reads *Règne de femmes*, which translates to Reign of Women.

Tucked underneath the overhang, a little farther up, is a directory for the police station, similar to the one at the Palais de Justice. From this we learn that Captain Renault's lair is on the building's ground floor. Here's the directory, again in English:

GROUND FLOOR
Office of the Prefect
Administrative Services
Passports-Visas
FIRST FLOOR
Criminal Investigation
National Safety
Identity-Fingerprints
SECOND FLOOR
Archives-Research
Pensions-Aged

Finally, up the street on the left is another perfume shop. The French sign out front informs us the shop is called Kiss of the Desert and features deluxe perfumes.

CLOSER LOOK: We spied at least three people in the crowd holding the same booklet. A later scene (we'll point it out when we get there) enables us to confirm that these booklets are meant to be passports issued by the French government.

RANDOM THOUGHTS: As market-goers glumly track the plane, Jan and Annina make another appearance. Despite everyone's depressed state, Annina cheerily hopes that they'll be on the same plane by tomorrow. Huh? Obviously she missed the Nazi swastika prominently displayed on the plane's tail. **(5:14)** The only place Jan and Annina would be going in that plane is back to Bulgaria.

Casablanca Airport

CLOSER LOOK: No one could mistake the plane shown mid-air for a real one. The special effects team created model versions of both planes featured in the film—this one and the one at the end of the film that departs for Lisbon.

But what about the plane shown taxiing on the tarmac? Now *that's* a real plane. Several distinguishing features confirm that it's a Super Universal made by the Fokker Aircraft Corp. The company began producing Super Universals in 1928. The planes held six passengers (four Reich officers deplane in the film) and two pilots and were commonly used by fledgling commercial airlines in the late 1920s and early 1930s.

JUST WONDERING?: Coming in for the landing, the plane flies over a sign for Rick's Café Américain, located atop a building. So is this supposed to mean that Rick's Café is near the airport? We will have our answer later tonight.

DID YOU KNOW?: The man behind Fokker Aircraft Corp. was famed Dutch airplane designer Anthony Fokker. Before World War I, Fokker pitched his airplane designs to all-comers and eventually convinced the German government that the airplane had value in military operations.

When World War I broke out in 1914, Germany was poised to make full use of Fokker's work. Among the planes Fokker delivered was the famed Dr.I triplane flown by German flying ace Manfred von Richthofen, better known as the Red Baron. Fokker also developed a gear-timing mechanism that allowed pilots to fire their machine guns through the plane's propeller without shredding it.

But in America Fokker lost his golden touch. In March 1931, with the Fokker company already getting crushed by the Great Depression (planes weren't exactly flying off the assembly line during this time), a Fokker commercial plane crashed after take-off from a Kansas City airport, killing all eight on board. Tragic yes, but plane crashes do happen from time to time, right?

Well, one of the plane's passengers was legendary Notre Dame football coach Knute Rockne, who was traveling to Hollywood to help in the production of the film *The Spirit of Notre Dame* (1931). Rockne's death assumed the status of national tragedy, and when the accident investigation determined that the crash was caused by a wing falling off for no good reason, Fokker's wood-constructed planes became an instant aeronautic pariah. Everybody, including Congress, wanted to question the man who designed the defective wing. With the Fokker name now linked to dodgy construction, the company's commercial airplane business was pretty well done.

EXPLANATION REQUIRED: One detail for the plane that had to be changed was its original registration markings. It's supposed to be a Nazi plane in Morocco, so it simply would not do to have the plane displaying its U.S. registration markings. No problem. The production team simply changed the markings to ones suitable for a German plane.

And impressively the plane's registration marking of D-AGDF is appropriate for a Nazi plane of that vintage. Since 1919 several countries, including Germany, had been using a five-letter plane identification scheme. The first letter identified the plane's country of origin, and one of the four letters that followed had to be a vowel. U.S.-registered planes had tail identifiers that started with N. Those registered in France had identifiers that started with F. Germany's identifier was D (for Deutschland).

RANDOM THOUGHTS: This whole matter of registration markings got us wondering about the history of this particular Fokker Super Universal, and whether it might still be around. Through some aviation-based forensics we discovered that the original U.S. registration marking for this particular plane was NC-9724. The plane was built in 1928, and during the 1930s it served as a commercial airliner for several companies before finding its way to Los Angeles Metropolitan Airport in 1942. There, it joined a stable of planes that were rented to film studios. So when it came time to film this scene in July 1942, NC-9724 was in the right place at the right time.

By all accounts NC-9724 should have enjoyed a long post-retirement career making film cameos. But we must report with great sadness that the plane's demise came just fifteen months after these scenes were shot. On October 10, 1943, a fire broke out in a hangar at the Los Angeles Metropolitan Airport. Destroyed in the fire were five planes, including NC-9724. So much for the nostalgic *Casablanca*-inspired flight we had hoped to take.

FILM ANECDOTES: A sign above the gate to the runway tells us this is the Casablanca Airport. **(5:17)** Of course, this is not the actual Casablanca airport that we are looking at here. Even if the budget-minded Warner Bros. wanted to film these scenes in Morocco, it could not have done so given that Casablanca was well within the sphere of World War II's North Africa Theater.

The obvious alternative was to use a Los Angeles-area airport, and of those the Los Angeles Metropolitan Airport in Van Nuys, California, was the best fit. This plucky little airport sprung up in 1928 as no more than a dirt strip in a sea of farmland. By year's end, the field sported an eye-catching Art Deco control tower and a couple of hangars. But the Great Depression took its toll, and the airport shuffled through the 1930s on a shoestring budget. The airport's owner worked in the film industry through most of the 1930s, and to generate extra revenue he hit on the idea of renting out the field to Hollywood studios.

All that came to an end in December 1941, when the United States entered World War II and the U.S. Army commandeered the field for the war effort. Not surprisingly, in July 1942, when these scenes were filmed, the Army was not entertaining on-location film shoot junkets. But Warner Bros. worked its connections with the Army and obtained permission to film not only this day scene but also a night scene, which appears at the end of the film and shows the Lisbon-bound plane on the runway.

DID YOU KNOW?: Look closely at the establishing shot and you'll notice a rather expansive tarmac and the ocean in the distance. But this is a scruffy little airport in Van Nuys, California, and Van Nuys is not seaside. So what gives? The answer is, of course, special effects.

The technique used here is called matte painting, which involves merging, through a double exposure, a live action scene (e.g., Major Strasser on the tarmac) with painted enhancements to the live scene (e.g., Casablanca cityscape and seascape). This is done by framing the scene and placing a glass plate in front of the camera lens that has been painted black or "matted" in the areas you want to fill in later. These matted areas don't get exposed on the negative.

Back at the studio you paint onto a glass sheet the scenes you want to appear in the matted area. Through a second exposure the painted areas are merged with the live action and, voilà, you have transformed a rural landlocked airport into one that plausibly looks like it's on the water's edge in Casablanca. A fairly inexpensive and straightforward process, with a big cinematic payoff.

CLOSER LOOK: So exactly what's real in this shot and what's been painted in? The control tower, hangars and building down the right side are all authentic, save for the building added just to the right of the control tower. (In the coming shots of the control tower notice that there's no terracotta-roofed building abutting on its right.) Also real is the foreground area as well as the strip of tarmac parallel to the buildings, where the plane taxis. The rest is filled in—the entire left side of the tarmac, the hangar on the left, the five planes parked on the tarmac, the array of buildings and, of course, the Atlantic Ocean.

RANDOM THOUGHTS: *Casablanca* is not the only film to make use of footage from the Los Angeles Metropolitan Airport. Here are a few films that include scenes filmed on the airport's grounds: Frank Capra's *Lost Horizon* (1938), *Storm Over the Andes* (1935) and *Men with Wings* (1938).

For the most part the footage in these films is confined to planes taxiing on the tarmac. But the Laurel and Hardy film short The *Flying Deuces* (1939) includes great shots of airport features. While being chased, the comic duo runs past and through two hangars visible in *Casablanca* before jumping into a plane and buzzing the control tower a few times.

CLOSER LOOK: Let's take the first of two closer looks at Major Strasser's uniform. The collar tabs—a single gull encircled by laurels—are fit for a major in the Luftwaffe. **(5:39)** Also visible on his hat and right chest is the Luftwaffe's iconic symbol, an eagle with a swastika dangling from its talons. And on the far right of his ribbon board we see Strasser's four- and twelve-year service awards.

EXPLANATION REQUIRED: As Strasser disembarks a French officer shouts in his native tongue, "Attention!" The French and Italian officers present do just that, and greet Strasser with a standard salute. Seconds later, Strasser and his countrymen exchange the infamous "Heil Hitler" salute.

EXPLANATION REQUIRED: Leading Strasser's greeting party is Herr Heinz. While Heinz's capacity is never discussed, we do learn later in the film that he's affiliated with the German Armistice Commission. We'll tell you how we know this, and explain the purpose of the commission, a little later.

Herr Heinz is not Luftwaffe material. His visor cap is army issue, with the cap's insignia tracking to actual German army cap variants.

Herr Heinz greets Strasser as *Major Strasser*. Actually, German military protocol would have had Strasser's subordinates referring to him as *Herr Major*. Indeed, at the end of the film, Herr Heinz does address Strasser as *Herr Major*. Strasser would have referred to the lesser-ranked Heinz as *Herr Heinz*. Strasser does not address Heinz by name, but Renault does introduce him as *Herr Heinz*. So while *Herr Heinz* always seemed a bit informal to us for military use, there is at least a basis for the reference.

FILM ANECDOTES: There has been some debate through the years as to whether any real airplane hangars appear in *Casablanca*. So let's take a look. First off, the hangar featured in the final scene definitely is not real. Those scenes (save a few snippets that we will discuss later) were shot entirely on Warner Bros. property.

The only other scene depicting hangars is the one at hand. When Strasser's plane lands two hangars are visible in the background. **(5:13)** While these hangars roughly match the ones that stood at the Los Angeles Metropolitan Airport at the time, it's obvious they are film artwork.

This brings us to the long shot of Strasser's plane taxiing on the tarmac. **(5:17)** To the right of Strasser's plane is the control tower and a line of buildings. After the first outbuilding are three hangars. Now *these* hangars are real and they are the only real ones that appear in the film.

CLOSER LOOK: So how do we know for sure these are actual hangars? Well, old photos, for one. But we also discovered a secret identifying mark. On the hangar nearest the control tower you can just make out the word AIRPORT on the hangar's roof. And sure enough, an old photo from the early 1940s confirms that at the time the hangar's roof read in full, LOS ANGELES METROPOLITAN AIRPORT, with AIRPORT appearing right where it does in the film. An exciting find, we say, but also a film gaffe—remember, we are supposed to be at an *AEROGARE* in French Morocco.

RANDOM THOUGHTS: So do the buildings that appear in this scene still exist? Well, first off, the airport is still around—it's now called the Van Nuys Airport, and from its bean field beginnings it grew into a seriously big general aviation airport, handling several hundred thousand takeoffs and landings annually. Unfortunately, the 50-foot stucco, architectural gem of a control tower, was torn down decades ago, a victim of airport expansion. Too bad, as it would have made for a wildly popular tourist attraction and the perfect host for a *Casablanca* exhibit.

Several sources indicate that one of the three hangars survives. Well, when we looked for ourselves years ago we were pleased to find a hanger standing in the same spot as one of the hangars shown in the film. It certainly looked the part with an arched roof and flanking corner piers.

But a few things about the structure had us puzzled. The doors just don't seem as tall as they appear in old photos, particularly in scenes from *The Flying Deuces*. The arch doesn't seem as prominent, and the door construction does not seem to match old photos. So either we are off base, or somewhere along the way, perhaps post-*Casablanca*, there was a rebuild on the same footprint or a rework of the door system or both. Whatever the case, just a year after we saw it a few industrious *Casablanca* fans saved the façade after the hangar was tagged for demolition. Word is they plan to incorporate the façade into a new hangar on airport grounds and create a *Casablanca*-themed establishment. Awesome idea and let's hope it happens.

CLOSER LOOK: Check out our map to see where the *Casablanca* scenes take place in relation to the airfield in its pre-World War II state. By the time *Casablanca's* on-location airport scenes were filmed in July 1942 the U.S. Army owned the place and was in the midst of an aggressive expansion that by September 1943 would have the place looking like a commercial airport. Still, the section of the field shown in these daytime shots had not changed much.

The Metro, as it was called before the Army purchased it, had three runways. The two longer ones were grass and ran north-south and east-west. A third oiled dirt runway ran northwest-southeast, paralleling the hangars visible in the film. A taxiway ran along side this third strip right in front of the hangars, and that is where we see Strasser's plane taxiing.

CASABLANCA AIRPORT

The Casablanca Airport illustration depicts the basic layout of the runways at the Los Angeles Metropolitan Airport before the Army started expansion work in 1942. Expansion was ongoing at the time the airport scenes were shot in the summer of 1942. We included in the illustration eight original structures—seven hangars and a control tower—all of which were still around at the time *Casablanca* was filmed. We also included two later addition buildings, both of which are visible in *Casablanca*. Filming was oriented along the southernmost east-west strip, which ran in front of a row of buildings comprised of: i) three hangars visible in the film; ii) one of the later addition buildings we just mentioned; and iii) the control tower.

1. Where Strasser's plane is shown just before landing, with arrow showing landing direction.
2. Airport control tower.
3. Where Strasser's plane is taxiing when first shown on the tarmac.
4. Where Strasser's plane is parked when Strasser deplanes.
5. Where Rick's Café should be located in relation to the airport based on Rick and Renault's view from the Café's terrace.
6. Where Rick's Café should be located in relation to the airport based on: i) the direction Strasser's plane lands; and ii) Strasser's plane passing over a sign for Rick's as it lands.
7. Where the Lisbon-bound plane is parked during the on-location shots at end of film.
8. The word AIRPORT is visible in the film on this hangar's roof; location of the hangar demolished in 2007 and thought to be the longest surviving airport structure visible in *Casablanca*.
9. The two later addition buildings; both are periodically visible in the background (one on either side of the control tower) when Renault greets Strasser and as the two make their way down the tarmac.

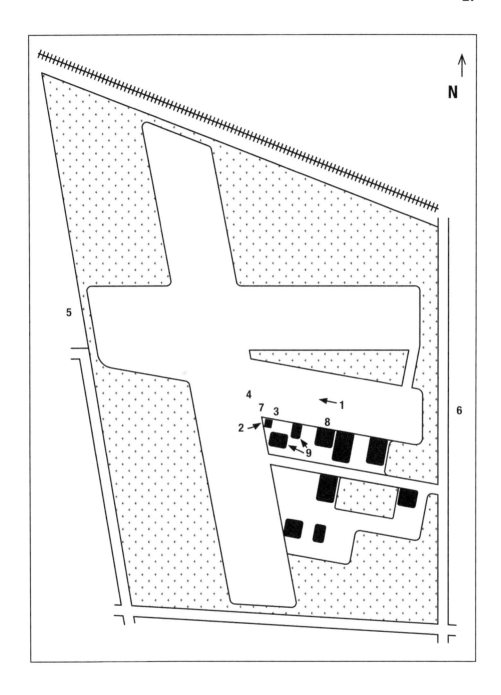

This taxiway is now a street called Waterman Drive. The street leads out to a public viewing area for the existing airport runway. If you are inspired to visit the site, the three hangars visible in *Casablanca* were on the south side of Waterman. The hangar discussed above was halfway down the street, just past the bend. The control tower stood at the end of the street on the south side, just short of the public viewing area. It's exciting to think that as you drive west down Waterman you are essentially re-tracing the path of Strasser's plane in the film.

FILM ANECDOTES: The half dozen or so palm trees swaying in the background in these shots had to have been brought in for filming. Old airport photos confirm that there were no palm trees in those areas. The trees were a good call as they help sell the exotic locale as well as the stifling African heat the director sought to convey.

CLOSER LOOK: Several film gaffes sprout up here of the scene inconsistency variety—ah, the challenges of on-location filming. One involves the random placement of equipment on the tarmac. In the establishing shot, which shows Strasser's plane taxiing, there are no planes or vehicles between Strasser's plane and the control tower. **(5:18)** But seconds later, as Strasser deplanes, a plane and fuel truck suddenly appear in front of the tower, with another plane parked nearby. **(5:41)** Well, oversights like this happen from time to time, right? But hold on here—a few seconds later things change again. As Strasser and Renault start walking, look for the fuel truck. It has moved a hundred feet or so, from in front of the tower to just behind the greeting party. **(6:26)** Now, someone on the production crew should have caught that one.

EXPLANATION REQUIRED: While on the tarmac we are treated to the first episode in an ongoing bit involving Renault's aide, Lieutenant Casselle, and a locally-based Italian officer, Captain Tonelli. The inspiration for this particular exchange is, of course, the fact that the Italian army was not particularly well respected either by the Germans or the Allies.

Here, Tonelli angles in front of a miffed Casselle to greet Strasser with much gusto and officialdom. Tonelli first states in English, "The Italian service, at your command, Major." After getting the brush off, Tonelli decides to lay some Italian on the major (though Strasser doesn't strike us as being up on his Romance languages), saying, "We have the great pleasure of your presence, Major. We are really happy to be at your service." But Strasser is not much interested in hearing from Captain Tonelli in any language.

Casselle sees all of this and mocks Tonelli in French, saying, "He doesn't even listen to you. I tell you that he doesn't even listen to you. You see!" Through this, Tonelli mumbles testily something like, "But for charity ...I do a favor." Poor Tonelli—it's going to be a long war for him and his countrymen.

DID YOU KNOW?: When Renault mentions that it's a trifle hot in Casablanca, Strasser boasts that Germans are used to adjusting to extreme weather conditions, from the plains of Russia to the deserts of North Africa. In fact, at that very moment, in December 1941, the German army was proving itself to be ill-equipped for winter warfare in Russia.

In the summer of 1941, Hitler ordered the invasion of Russia, and banked on wrapping things up by fall. Having caught the Russians by surprise, the Germans had the early upper-hand and Hitler's plan looked to be on course. But the Russians regrouped, and as the weeks wore on the Germans soon found themselves fighting a winter war in their summer uniforms. The Russians were used to fighting in harsh conditions, and in the first week of December 1941, shortly after the Germans reached Moscow, they leveraged their abundance of winterized clothing and equipment into a winter counter-offensive that sent the Germans into partial retreat.

CLOSER LOOK: An Air France fuel truck is parked on the tarmac. Signage on the side of the truck translates to Regular Gas for Airplanes. Also visible is a very sensible warning (*Défense de Fumer*) not to smoke near the truck.

CLOSER LOOK: It's the smallest of details, but the flag flying atop the gate to the tarmac is a head scratcher. A Moroccan or Casablancan flag? Or something related to the war? Actually, it's an Air France flag. Of course, this makes sense knowing that the Air France name also appears above the gate (not visible in the film) and on the sides of the gate (partially visible), meaning that this is supposed to be the Air France terminal. **(5:20)** Anyway, the key to figuring out that the flag belongs to Air France is the logo in the flag's center, which appears more prominently later in the film. We'll talk more about this when the time comes.

DID YOU KNOW?: Air France was founded in 1933, and by the time World War II broke out the airline was a major player in the European commercial airline market. It does make sense that Air France is featured in the film. While the war forced Air France to continually adjust its service, the airline did maintain flights to Casablanca.

CLOSER LOOK: Two men on the tarmac are charged with opening the plane door and gathering passenger luggage. In the establishing shot, of the thirty-four greeters visible, these two are farthest to the right. In the next shot, they dash to the plane. The wheelbarrow-style cart then appears behind Strasser and Renault as they first speak. Look for the French word for luggage, *bagages*, on the side of the cart. The front of the cart reads Air

France; you can only see the last two letters in *France* in the film. This cart shows up in the final scene, with Victor and Ilsa's luggage on it, rolling in the background as Rick sets Victor straight.

CLOSER LOOK: The four soldiers guarding the arched gate to the tarmac appear to be Senegalese Tirailleurs, which is an actual French corps made up of soldiers recruited not only from Senegal but also other territories in French West Africa. Tirailleurs (*tirailleur* means sharpshooter in French) wore a distinctive red fez, and khaki shorts were definitely in play due to the heat. Four more Tirailleurs are on the tarmac, visible behind Strasser and Renault as they walk. While all eight sport rifles, the four on the tarmac have their bayonets attached.

CLOSER LOOK: Captain Tonelli is not the only Italian on the tarmac. A second officer, who appears to be his aide, is by Tonelli's side throughout the scene. The aide's visor cap has two stripes, which means he's a lieutenant. Tonelli's cap has three stripes, which is appropriate for a captain. Tonelli's cap insignia is for a cavalry regiment, and the number encircled at the bottom tells us he's in the 1st regiment. His aide's cap insignia resembles that of an Italian naval officer of his rank.

CLOSER LOOK: All right, just a few more pieces of aviation-based forensics before we head over to Rick's for some cocktails. For this we must back up a bit to the very first shot of the control tower and Strasser's taxiing plane.

First, look in the lower right corner for the wing of a plane and the plane's registration marking, 972Y. **(5:18)** Any chance that it's a real registration marking? You bet! Registration NC-972Y was assigned in 1928 to a plane made by Lockheed called a Vega C5. And guess what? There is no doubt from this shot, and another one showing Strasser and Renault walking on the tarmac, that this plane is a Vega C5. We love it when these things check out. But we would be remiss if we did not point out that the production team missed one here. A U.S.-registered Lockheed Vega sitting on the tarmac in Morocco? Possible, but not likely.

Finally, the sleek two-seater next to it appears to be a prototype B-3 Super Sport made by Brown Aircraft Company, which specialized in planes built for speed and competitive racing. The plane would have had registration markings assigned to it, but they either were covered up for the shoot or previously removed. Brown never made a production version due to lack of demand.

RANDOM THOUGHTS: So while we now know the Super Universal no longer exists, any chance NC-972Y is still around? Well, we told you earlier that the Super Universal was lost in a hangar fire in October 1943, along with four other planes. Turns out that NC-972Y was one of the four other planes. So we will not be taking a *Casablanca*-inspired joyride in this plane either.

FILM ANECDOTES: After an awesome teaser line like "Everybody comes to Rick's," there is no way that the *next* scene could take place anywhere but Rick's Café, right? Well, that wasn't how things stood heading into filming. Instead, wedged in between the airport scene and our introduction to Rick's Café was a daytime scene that took place at a Moorish hotel called Hotel Hemen. The purpose of the scene was to introduce Victor Laszlo and reveal his mission in Casablanca.

Here's how the scene was to fit in. At the airport, Strasser and Renault discuss not only the murder of the couriers, but also Victor Laszlo surfacing in Casablanca. Then, cutting to Hotel Hemen, Victor asks a woman at the front desk about a man named Señor Ugarte. At first the woman is guarded, but then she sees Victor's business card and tells Victor he can find Ugarte at Rick's around 10:00 p.m. After Victor leaves, papers visible behind the front desk bear the Cross of Lorraine, indicating that Hotel Hemen has ties to the French Resistance.

Eliminating this scene seems to have been a good call under the "more is less" theory. The scene definitely would have been a momentum killer, and whatever set-up value it had is accomplished by Victor in just a few lines upon his arrival at Rick's.

CHAPTER 2

EVERYBODY COMES TO RICK'S

"Waiting, waiting, waiting. I'll never get out of here.
I'll die in Casablanca."
— Patron in Rick's

Nightfall in Casablanca brings some welcome relief from the stifling heat that greeted Major Strasser and his entourage on the tarmac. But things are about to heat up in a different way at the city's liveliest night spot, Rick's Café Américain.

It appears that Captain Renault knew of what he spoke. Everybody really *does* come to Rick's. And why not—it has something for everyone. The place has an air of sophistication, yet it's decidedly unpretentious. One can just as comfortably saddle up at the bar for a couple of stiff ones as order champagne and caviar at a private table for two. Sam, the house tunester, does his best to boost spirits by playing the latest feel-good hits.

And the clientele? Eclectic, to be sure. Here, the social elite mingle with murderers, thieves and opportunists. Germans, French, Italians, Brits, Americans, Spaniards, Czechs, Bulgarians, Norwegians, Russians, Moroccans, Chinese—you name it, they're all here. Nearly all against their will, trying to make the best of a bad situation.

Considering the circumstances, people get along fairly well, though there is the occasional and inevitable patriotism-induced altercation. Soldiers mix with the very refugees they're oppressing. Thieves and cheats ply their trade right under the noses of the authorities. But inside Rick's, everyone seems resigned to taking time off from the madness, if only to down a few drinks in relative calm.

Our tour then of Rick's begins in the main room. Cutting through the din we eavesdrop on various conversations that together give us a good sense of what Rick's is all about. The common thread in these conversations is that *everyone* wants to get out of Casablanca.

Carl the waiter escorts us from the main room to a semi-private one, and we are not at all shocked to find that gambling is going on in there.

The room is a more upscale affair that allows the sifted ones to make their inevitable donations to the house in style and comfort.

Alone at a table playing chess sits the establishment's owner and namesake, one Richard Blaine. Straight away Rick denies entry to a well-to-do pro-German patron. Message received. Nothing happens in Rick's without his permission.

Now that we have a feel for how things work at Rick's, it's time to revisit the plot. A regular named Ugarte joins Rick at his table. Even before Ugarte refers to himself as a "parasite" it's clear he skews toward the shady side. Ugarte, so he says, is on the verge of his greatest moment. Remember those two letters of transit? Well, "somehow" they have fallen into his possession. But he's feeling the heat from the German authorities, and figures that Rick's is the perfect temporary safe house for the letters.

Now Rick strikes us as the kind of guy who would have zero tolerance for Ugarte's hare-brained schemes. But surprisingly, despite a stream of snarky comments directed at Ugarte, Rick agrees to hold the letters, if only for the evening. Now the question becomes where to stash them. Of his many choices, Rick opts to slip them inside the top of Sam's piano, mid-song.

With the letters of transit safely tucked away, Rick lingers in the main room and in short order runs into Signor Ferrari, his cross-town rival in the bar business. Polite chitchat quickly turns to a standing offer from Ferrari to buy Rick's Café, Sam included. Ferrari runs the black market in town and is both impressed and dismayed by the inroads Rick has made on his business. Having sized up Rick as long-term competition, Ferrari tries to buy his way out of the matter. But while nearly everything in Casablanca is for sale—even humans, as Ferrari points out—the Café is not. Not just yet anyway.

With this curious business exchange behind him, Rick seeks sanctuary at the bar only to get blindsided by Yvonne, freshly jilted by Rick. Rick has no time for Yvonne's theatrics and sends her home rather roughly. The exchange creates the impression that women do not get the upperhand on Rick.

Well, all of this excitement—the stealthy deals, the weighty business propositions, the love-spurning encounters—has Rick in need of a ciggy and a breath of fresh air, so he makes his way to the terrace. There he runs into Captain Renault, who in a relaxed but pointed manner starts probing Rick's psyche. Why is Rick here in Casablanca, Renault wants to know. Is Rick on the run? Is he a thief, a paramour, a murderer? A combination of all three? None of the above? Who can really tell, what with Rick's maddeningly evasive responses. The only thing we *do* know is that with each moment Rick is proving himself to be quite the enigma.

Rick's—Main Room

CLOSER LOOK: The neon sign above the Café's entrance matches the design of the one we just saw Strasser's plane fly over. Different signs, but with the same script and outline.

MUSIC NOTES: Our arrival at Rick's could not be better timed. Just as we enter, house musician Sam slips into a lively version of "It Had to Be You." Warner Bros. didn't have to go far to fetch this 1924 classic as it was already in its music library. The studio had acquired the rights to the song in the late 1920s, when film studios were snapping up music publishers to meet the increased demand for music driven by the arrival of talking pictures.

To be sure the song's melody has a romantic quality, but the lyrics? Listen for yourself, but fairly summarized the message from this love serenade is: "Sure, I've had a lot of lovers in my time, but none of them could cure my wandering eye until you. I don't even care that you put me in a serious funk, or that you're riddled with faults or that you're mean, cross and bossy. You're the only one for me." Hmmm. On closer look, not exactly wedding "first dance" material.

MUSIC NOTES: After "It Had to Be You," Sam segues into a whimsical number called "Shine," featuring some mildly provocative race-based humor. This song was written in 1910 by an African-American duo, and is thought to be inspired by a real-life New York City neighborhood character who got caught up in the race riots in the summer of 1900. Louis Armstrong popularized the song in the 1930s, and, taking a page out of Armstrong's book, Sam works the crowd nicely through a healthy dose of feel-good mugging. Here are the lyrics heard during this scene:

> *Cause, my hair is curly*
> *Ohhhh, my teeth are pearly.*
> *Just because I always wear a smile,*
> *Like to dress up in the latest style.*
>
> *'Cause, I'm glad I'm living.*
> *Take troubles smiling, never whine.*
> *Just because my color's shady, a bit different maybe*
> *That's why they call me*
> *That's why they call me 'Shine.'*

RICK'S CAFÉ—FIRST NIGHT

Here's the first of two Rick's Café illustrations. Both use our custom rendering of the Café, with this one detailing Café activity on the first night. The stairs show how Rick's apartment and office tie into the main room. The second floor landing outside Rick's apartment doubles as a balcony overlooking the main room. Underneath the balcony is a passageway that runs from the main room to the gambling room entrance.

1. Sam playing opening songs, "It Had to Be You" and "Shine"; also "Knock on Wood."
2. House band.
3. Patron at table saying, "Waiting, waiting, waiting. I'll never get out of here. I'll die in Casablanca."
4. Woman at table selling diamond bracelet.
5. Men at table playing dominos, with one saying, "The trucks are waiting, the men are waiting."
6. Man at table providing instructions for meeting a boat.
7. Rick hides letters of transit in piano during "Knock on Wood."
8. Ferrari's table.
9. Yvonne and Sascha at bar, then Rick joins.
10. Where Rick takes Yvonne to get her coat after their words at the bar.
11. Rick and Renault on terrace; also where Victor and Ilsa enter cab.
12. Sam singing "Baby Face."
13. Strasser and Herr Heinz's table, with Renault joining, then Rick.
14. Where Ugarte pleads with Rick for help.
15. Victor and Ilsa's table (table moves around shot-to-shot, but stays in same general area); also where Sam and Ilsa convene, with Sam playing "Avalon" and "As Time Goes By"; also where Victor, Ilsa, Strasser and Renault talk at end of night.
16. Victor meets with fellow Resistance member Berger at the bar, then Renault joins.
17. Señorita Andreya singing "Tango Delle Rose."
18. Rick's table for Paris flashback and ensuing talk with Ilsa.

37

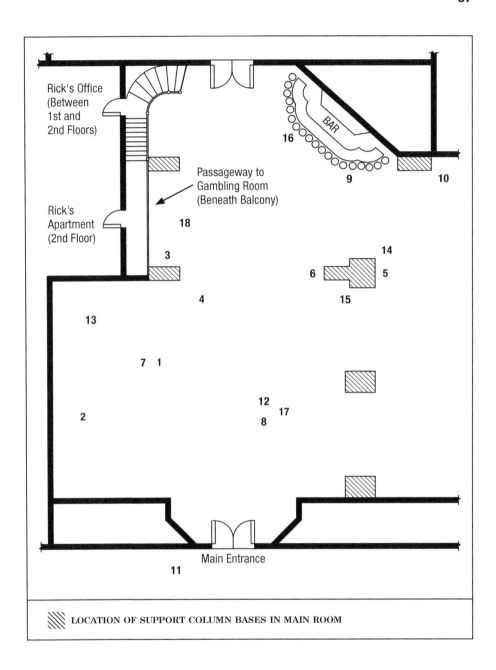

LOCATION OF SUPPORT COLUMN BASES IN MAIN ROOM

CLOSER LOOK: In a shadowy nook of Rick's main room sits a man smoking a hookah; that is to say, a water pipe. An employee delivers a fruit bowl and then tends to the man's hookah, perhaps to refill it with tobacco. The hookah, known as a shisha in Morocco, is believed to have its origins in India, but it's hard to say for sure. What is certain is that the Turks embraced it like no other and made it a permanent part of their social fabric.

The hookah's key feature is a glass water chamber on the bottom—the smoke filters through water, so that when you inhale your lungs don't catch fire. Notwithstanding its historical ties to hashish and opium, the hookah is primarily used for smoking fruit-flavored tobacco. Since Rick's is a reputable joint we're betting against this patron partaking in the illicit stuff here.

The hookah's presence in the Café is questionable—they weren't exactly mainstream in Casablanca back then and, in any event, wouldn't be used publicly like this. Even so, this guy is breaching long-standing hookah etiquette by resting it on a ledge. In various corners of the world it is considered very bad manners to place the hookah anywhere but on the ground. So lesson learned—keep the hubbly-bubbly off the table.

RANDOM THOUGHTS: The first in a series of vignettes representing the goings-on at the Café features a despondent man who is convinced he will never get out of Casablanca. But as we will soon see, escaping Casablanca is really just a function of money. So if this guy would stop hanging out at Rick's every night running up hefty bar bills, he'd be in Lisbon in no time.

CLOSER LOOK: In the next vignette we find a woman trying to hock a diamond bracelet. A local diamond broker uses a jeweler's loupe to examine the piece. If he likes what he sees, he's not telling, and offers the woman a mere 2,400 francs for what looks like a pretty nice piece. Sorry, but 2,400 francs, around $60 in 1941 U.S. dollars, ain't gonna be enough to buy passage out of Casablanca. And it's clear from this woman's demeanor that she knows it. Her lifeless stare is telling—she never even blinks. Notice she's not wearing a necklace or earrings, creating the impression they went first. As she reflexively fiddles with her ring, we get the feeling she's going to be parting with it as well. **(7:40)**

DID YOU KNOW?: The broker complains that diamonds are everywhere, which may be true in Rick's where folks are selling anything and everything to fund an exit visa. But interestingly, from a geological perspective, he's also correct. To the surprise of many, diamonds are not at all a scarce commodity. In fact, great caches of diamonds pepper the world—South Africa, Brazil, Borneo, Canada, Siberia, Australia—belched up in magma from a hundred or so miles below the earth's surface through pipes known as kimberlites. Head to aptly-named Kimberley, South Africa, and you'll find what's known as the Big Hole, a kimberlite that between 1871 and 1914 was mined to a depth of over two thousand feet, while producing some 14 million carats of diamonds.

So why are diamonds so expensive? In a word, *cartel*. Turns out, the diamond industry makes for a fascinating case study in the otherwise yawn-inducing topic of economics. It seems that for more than a century a South African conglomerate known commonly as De Beers has led both the mining and distribution of diamonds, making price control a function of restricting inventory. And through the decades, with each new diamond mine discovered, DeBeers had output funneling through its distribution channels, keeping the market from flooding. On the demand side, in the 1940s De Beers funded an ingenious marketing campaign aimed at convincing Americans that a diamond was the exclusive symbol of betrothal, and eventually hit on one of the all-time great ad slogans, Diamonds Are Forever.

During World War II, DeBeers' market position was so strong that it did not feel at all compelled to meet the United States' war needs. Being one seriously hard substance, diamond has a host of industrial applications such as cutting, grinding and polishing. As manufacturing ramped up on both sides during the war, the demand for diamonds went through the roof. The Germans had a decent supply through various mines they controlled in Africa, but the Allies were not as well positioned. Despite the obvious urgency, De Beers' fear of flooding the market led it to withhold supply from the U.S. government. Only after the United States threatened to withhold essential war supplies from Great Britain did De Beers agree to cough up the carbon.

CAST ANECDOTES: Just a year after making *Casablanca*, German actress Lotte Palfi, who plays the diamond-hocking refugee, married fellow *Casablanca* actor Wolfgang Zilzer. We saw Zilzer in an earlier scene playing the man gunned down in the market during the refugee round-up. This is one of two *Casablanca* marriage connections. We'll clue you in to the other *Casablanca* couple (who actually were seeking a divorce during filming) a little later.

Look for Palfi in a nice World War II spy thriller *Above Suspicion* (1943, also with Conrad Veidt and Ludwig Stossel) as an Austrian bookstore clerk with Nazi leanings. Zilzer can be found in *All Through the Night* (1942), playing a Nazi spy and sharing a scene with Conrad Veidt and Peter Lorre as fellow spies. And both Palfi and Zilzer appear in *Confessions of a Nazi Spy* (1939), though not together, with Palfi playing a nurse and Zilzer a less-than-confident spy.

EXPLANATION REQUIRED: Eavesdropping on two men discussing an illicit transaction, one explains to the other that the trucks and the men are waiting. But before we learn who is waiting and what they are waiting for, two Germans walk within earshot, and the men go silent. One of the Germans, apparently not happy with the fast-and-loose atmosphere in Rick's, comments to the other in his native tongue, "I don't understand the whole thing—one should have a much stronger hand here in Casablanca." **(7:43)** Surely, then, they'll be pleased to learn that the iron-fisted Major Strasser has arrived.

DID YOU KNOW?: These two men finalize their scheme over a game of dominoes; it's a popular game among Europeans, so it's not surprising to see these two transplants playing here. It looks like they're playing a game of Block or Draw, though it doesn't make sense that the tiles in the side-pile are face up. High level, these games involve players drawing tiles for their hand and then taking turns playing tiles by matching numbers. Not exactly heady stuff but when you're stuck in Casablanca most anything will do to pass the time. Whatever the game, the men have already played a few tiles, and the one with his back to us has six left in his hand. **(7:47)**

CLOSER LOOK: At another table a refugee smuggling transaction appears to be at hand. The broker tells the refugee that his ticket out of town is the *Santiago*, a boat that will sail from Casablanca tomorrow night. The refugee has a spot on it, but only if he brings 15,000 francs, in cash.

A few things to point out here. First, the broker refers to the boat as a "fishing smack," which is a type of fishing boat propelled by sails. If the *Santiago* is headed for Portugal, it's going to be a long and rough ride. Second, the broker cleverly uses a house menu to obscure a slip of paper containing the instructions.

Third, a casual listen might have you thinking the boat is leaving from the end of *the marina*, which certainly makes sense. But the film script has it that the *Santiago* is leaving from the "end of La Medina," which would be a reference to the city's old quarter. Interesting. Well, in fact Casablanca's medina is down by the harbor, so technically this reference holds up. But it's a good-sized harbor and with no further instructions we're a little worried the refugee won't be able to find the boat.

Finally, just asking, but under the circumstances is there really any legitimate payment option besides cash?

CAST ANECDOTES: If you're a fan of *It's a Wonderful Life* (1946), the actor playing the black-market visa broker, William Edmunds, should look familiar to you. Edmunds played the colorful Mr. Martini in that holiday film classic. He typically played affable foreign gents, so you might say this darker role—all eight seconds of it anyway—was somewhat of a break-out performance for him. Edmunds was born in Italy and, while he most often played Italian and Spanish characters, in *Casablanca* there's no hint as to his heritage.

RANDOM THOUGHTS: Doing some more number crunching, back in 1941 15,000 francs converted to around $375. That amount in 1941 is equivalent in purchasing power to around $6,300 today.

Given that the price for freedom is not cheap, this refugee better make sure he's on the boat before he hands over the cash. During the World War II many boat smuggling propositions of this nature were outright cons. Countless refugees paid upfront money only to find themselves stranded dockside waiting for a never-to-be-seen-again captain.

EXPLANATION REQUIRED: So far *Casablanca* is proving to be a multilingual affair, with smatterings of French, Italian and German dialogue. Now, just after the fishing smack exchange, two rather more challenging languages pop up. First, on the way to the bar two men speak in hushed Chinese, and more specifically Cantonese. As with everyone else in the Café tonight, they too have an illicit scheme in the works. The snippet of Cantonese that we overhear translates to, "Don't worry. I've arranged everything. It is well arranged." **(8:01)** We're going to take a wild guess that he's referring to yet another exit visa transaction hosted by Rick's.

Next, we arrive at the bar in time to observe a brief exchange between Sascha the Russian bartender and a thirsty British patron. The first part of Sascha's Russian toast is a traditional one that basically means, "To your health." The second part is not so much a toast as a dare, and means, "Drink to the bottom!" Getting the gist of Sascha's pleasantry, the Brit returns the favor with a toast from his country, "Cheerio!" If he's going to take Sascha's dare and down that tall cocktail in one gulp, he'd do well to lose the straw.

FILM ANECDOTES: One vignette slated to appear in this montage did not make it past the film censors. It had a beautiful young woman sitting at a table with an older man, reflecting nostalgically, "It used to take a villa at Cannes, or the very least, a string of pearls. Now all I ask is an exit visa." Hmmm. That does not sound like the standard cash-for-visa transaction we're used to seeing in Rick's.

Rick's—Gambling Room

EXPLANATION REQUIRED: Stationed at the entrance to the gambling room is Abdul, one of the Café's doormen. His fez, our sources tell us, is more Egyptian than Moroccan. His vest is adorned with embroidery one might find on traditional Moroccan clothing. The harem pants are a pure Hollywood embellishment.

Carl the waiter asks Abdul to open the door, prompting Abdul to refer to Carl as "Herr Professor." So why does Abdul call Carl "Professor"? An earlier version of the script included a scene just before Abdul and Carl's exchange. That scene had Sascha the bartender explaining to a customer that before the war Carl was a professor at the University of Leipzig, and had written books on mathematics and astronomy. Cutting this vignette left Abdul's comment with no context. Hey, nobody said film editing was easy.

CLOSER LOOK: One gets the impression that only a few seconds lapse from the time Carl enters the gambling room to the time he reaches the table of card players. But a longer lapse of time is the only way to avoid concluding that another continuity gaffe occurs here. That's because when Carl heads into the room he's carrying a tray with two cocktails, but when he arrives at the table he doesn't have the tray. Instead, Carl serves coffee off another server's tray.

CLOSER LOOK: Carl delivers drinks to some inquisitive gamblers, who pump him for information on Rick and his peculiar ways. If they're playing poker then the smart money is on the woman on the left. She appears to be holding a full house—two 10s and three jacks. **(8:49)**

RANDOM THOUGHTS: One gambling patron is offended that Rick refuses to join them and wryly asks Carl to inform Rick that he runs the second largest bank in Amsterdam. Carl responds, tongue-in-cheek, that Rick wouldn't be impressed because the head of the *largest* Amsterdam bank works in Rick's kitchen...and his father works as a bellboy. Everyone gets a good laugh, and it's a funny line to be sure. But for the record, we must point out that Rick's is a café, not a hotel. Perhaps Carl should have said bus boy.

CLOSER LOOK: As Rick plays a little solitaire chess, a staff member asks him to authorize a gambling voucher. We get a glimpse of the voucher, but it's not enough time to take it all in. So here's a mock-up of the form, with the filled-in portions omitted:

```
RICK'S                                          Fcs.
CAFE AMERICAIN

Bon pour une avance de Francs Marocains: _____

Au bénéfice de M _____
Remboursable le_____
                          Casablanca, le _____
Autorisation              Commissaire des Jeux

_____          _____
                    Caissier
                 _____
```

From the filled in portions we learn that on December 2, 1941, Rick's is advancing 1,000 Moroccan francs to a female patron, to be repaid by her that same day—hey, tough times call for tough terms. In addition to the authorization line that Rick signs, the voucher includes sign-off lines for the Commissioner of Games and a cashier. Also, in the lower left corner there's a signature and some writing, which together reads to us as someone's acceptance.

CAST ANECDOTES: Bogart looks quite comfortable in front of a chessboard, with his casual yet thoughtful handling of pieces; and with good reason. He was an avid chess player, and a talented one at that. While scraping by as a stage actor in New York, Bogart is said to have supplemented his income playing chess for money.

Certainly throughout his film career a chessboard was never far from reach on the set. Bogart regularly squared off with fellow actors, including Sidney Greenstreet and Paul Henreid on the set of *Casablanca*.

Bogart was sufficiently immersed in the West Coast chess scene that in 1945 he and his wife, Lauren Bacall, appeared on the cover of the magazine *Chess Review* to promote a Pan-American chess tournament being held in Los Angeles. The cover featured Bogart and Charles Boyer studying their next moves in between takes during the filming of *Confidential Agent* (1945), with Bacall and renowned chess master Herman Steiner board-side. Steiner, who was the host of the aforementioned tournament, was close with Bogart and regularly gave lessons to Hollywood stars. To see Bogart studying a chess position in another film check out the beginning of *Knock On Any Door* (1949).

FILM ANECDOTES: While Bogart, Henreid and Greenstreet were chess aficionados, *Casablanca* actors Conrad Veidt (Major Strasser) and Peter Lorre (Ugarte) enjoyed the less serious game of table tennis. These two knew each other from their German movie days. And while working on a film together in 1932 they discovered that, despite their considerable height difference—Veidt at 6' 3" and Lorre at 5' 5"—they made a formidable team.

CLOSER LOOK: Back at Rick's table there are several continuity gaffes to point out—not all that surprising given the multitude of props in play. In the first shot of the chessboard, an ashtray sits between Rick and his champagne glass. **(8:52)** But in the next shot—with Rick only having signed the voucher in between—the glass is now on Rick's side of the ashtray, and much closer to the edge of the board. **(9:01)** Also, the second shot shows two captured bishops board-side, one white piece and one black piece, with Rick touching the closer white piece. But in the previous shot the two pieces appear to be reversed. Next, the writing on the voucher in the close-up shot differs ever so slightly from the writing visible when Rick hands it back to the staff member. Finally, Rick's left hand steadies the voucher as he signs, but in the next shot it's not there.

JUST WONDERING: Is that really Bogart signing the voucher, or could it be the work of a hand double? Bogart wears a ring on the ring finger of his right hand in this scene and throughout the film. But in this shot the ring finger is not visible. Absent that confirming visual, we say the hand looks a little too youthful to be Bogart's.

DID YOU KNOW?: We were supremely pleased to find that Rick is indeed overseeing a legitimate chess match. Just after Rick signs the voucher we get a view of the board that enables us to diagram the game. Here is how things stood through Rick's last move of a White knight, made just after he signs the voucher:

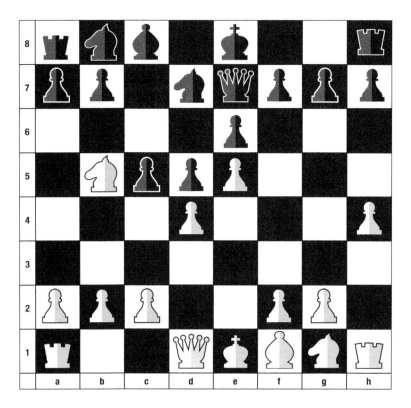

Turns out this is not just any chess game. For those of you not up on your chess strategies, the board layout confirms that Rick is playing for Black a variation of an established opening to a chess match known as the French Defense. Whoa! *The French Defense*?! Looks like Bogart and the prop team had fun here, engaging in some World War II chess symbolism. Given France's present wartime predicament, it's the perfect choice for a board configuration. Most interestingly, one common line of the French Defense features the exchange of bishops early on, and indeed just moments ago we saw that Rick had removed from the board both a White and Black bishop. **(9:04)**

CLOSER LOOK: Continuity relating to the chess board is pretty good throughout the scene, but there are some issues. Stick with us here as we walk through the sequence.

First, Rick contemplates moving a White knight, and we can see that the move contemplated is from square c3 to b5. But in the previous (and first) shot of the board that knight is already on b5. After Rick allows entry to the party of three, we see a shot of the board that confirms that Rick did end up moving that knight to b5, which is where it remains for all subsequent shots.

Second, the shot in which Rick moves the White knight has different positioning for Black than the next shot, the one in which Rick nods in the party of three. In the former, Black's king is in its starting position; in the latter, it has moved left, to the other side of the king-side rook. **(9:11)** Now, the king could have legitimately ended up there through what is known in chess parlance as a "castling" maneuver, but, being true to the shot sequence, Rick didn't have enough time to make the move.

Moving along, in the next shot of the board—showing Rick denying access to a man—the Black king is back to its pre-castling position. **(9:22)** Hmmm. What is going on here? In the next shot of the board—showing Rick back at the table with Ugarte—Rick's first move is to make that castling maneuver for Black. **(10:22)** Thereafter, all shots show Black in a castling position.

And just when it appears that everything is back on track, continuity issues pop up with White again. The White bishop shown captured was the queen-side bishop. But, bizarrely, in all shots of the board after Ugarte joins Rick, White's remaining bishop is no longer the king-side bishop; rather, the queen-side bishop is the one left on the board.

Finally, as Ugarte explains that the letters of transit cannot be rescinded, White's king-side rook has disappeared from its starting position and appears to be off the board, next to Ugarte's left hand. Yep, the rook was in its starting position before and after this shot.

While the board continuity issues involving Black's king could be attributable to shuffling scenes that were shot out of sequence, switching White bishops and leaving a rook off the board for a single shot appear to be plain old oversights, and ones that Bogart himself should have caught.

FILM ANECDOTES: In 2014, a piece of Bogart memorabilia came up for auction—a letter describing Bogart's next chess move in a so-called mail correspondence chess match. The stated provenance for the letter was that the match occurred during the filming of *Casablanca*, with the auction house suggesting that the board in the film reflects the match referenced in the letter.

Whatever the case, correspondence matches were common back in the day, and Bogart seemed to particularly enjoy them. During World War II, Bogart played correspondence chess with G.I.'s as a way to support the troops. If you think chess calls for patience, try waiting a few weeks for a letter to come by snail mail with you opponent's latest inspired advance of a pawn one square.

DID YOU KNOW?: Not everyone has what it takes to gain access to the Café's back room. Rick allows a party of three to enter, but then stiffs the next man. Ugarte implies that he's a Deutsche Bank executive, which would be quite surprising given that the man does not have even a hint of a German accent. The man is sufficiently outraged that he promises to report the incident to "the Angriff."

Well, it turns out that this was no small threat. *Der Angriff* was a Nazi Party newspaper, an early vehicle for delivering propaganda and messages of hate to the German people. The paper was founded in 1927 (several years before the Nazi Party assumed power) by Joseph Goebbels, who for years served as Hitler's chief propagandist. The newspaper was a key force behind the rise of the party. And lest there be any doubt as to what Geobbels' paper was all about, *angriff* means *attack* in German. Yikes! Careful Rick, these Germans are known for their reprisals.

CAST ANECDOTES: Speaking of Nazi propaganda, at least three *Casablanca* cast members—Peter Lorre, Curt Bois and Marcel Dalio—found themselves exploited in Nazi anti-Semitic propaganda campaigns. The Nazis referenced Bois, Lorre and several other Jewish celebrities (mainly through archival footage) in a deplorable 1940 Nazi anti-Semitic pseudo-documentary.

Equally harrowing, in the summer of 1940 the Germans hung posters of Dalio around Paris with captioning along the lines of "A Typical Jew." We haven't been able to track down the poster, and it seems that not even Dalio saw it since he had already fled Paris (more on this shortly). But according to Dalio, a friend relayed to him that the Germans had hung the aforementioned posters all along Paris' Avenue de l'Opéra. Years later Dalio wryly mused that he had no idea he would some day be charged with responsibility for the decline of the West.

So how did Dalio manage to become the subject of a Nazi anti-Semitic poster campaign? Well, apart from him being a celebrity and Jewish, he appeared in a film reviled by the party called *La Grande Illusion* (1937). The Nazis hated this film for its less-than-flattering portrayal of Germans and premise of French political and social superiority; so much so that they banned it and sought to destroy all copies. Dalio's appearance in the film was bad enough from the Nazi's perspective, but the kicker was that he played a Jewish prisoner of war who outfoxes the Germans by escaping from a prison that the Germans had declared escape proof.

CLOSER LOOK: The actress playing the woman Rick just allowed into the gambling room appears to have lucked into two roles for this first night at the Café. We'll point her out when she appears a few scenes from now, hanging out the in main room and wearing a far more casual outfit. Meanwhile, her regal, medieval-esque headdress fits in nicely with the high-class scene in the gambling room. No wonder Rick waved her in.

RANDOM THOUGHTS: We know Ugarte is in illegal possession of the letters of transit, but the film implies that Ugarte is guilty of the higher crime of murdering the German couriers. But consider whether he is merely a patsy, fingered by Captain Renault for the murders. Two things point in this direction. First, Renault is under extreme pressure to solve the crime. Arresting a black marketeer like Ugarte will not be second-guessed, and doing so on the quick will earn Renault a feather in his kepi in the eyes of Strasser.

Second, Renault has a financial motive. While defending his black-market sales practices to Rick, Ugarte says, "But think of all the poor devils who can't meet *Renault's* price. Well, I get it for them for half." Interesting. We later learn that Renault has a habit of trading exit visas for female companionship. So it's clear that Renault's connections to the black market run deep. And by pinning the murders on Ugarte, Renault instantly eliminates his chief competition, which means more black-market revenue to fund his vices.

CLOSER LOOK: No scam, it seems, is below the resourceful Ugarte. As he explains his plan to Rick, Ugarte has a couple of drinks on Rick's dime. Just as he receives the first one, he puts in an order for the second. He then dashes off with that drink without bothering to finish the first. Now, that's the mark of a professional parasite—doubling up on drinks after inviting yourself to the owner's table.

EXPLANATION REQUIRED: Hearing Ugarte's bizarre accent we wondered where he's from. His bidding of "Addio" to Casablanca points to Italian. But in the original play his first name was Guillermo, which is Spanish, and the surname Ugarte has roots in Basque Country. Further digging reveals that his use of Italian was not an oversight. Industry censors suggested that Warner Bros. portray Ugarte as Italian rather than Spanish so as not to offend folks in war-neutral countries in Latin America. And making a seedy character like Ugarte the a citizen of an Axis member was a nifty fix. Whatever the case, to Ugarte we will shortly be saying, "Goodbye!"

RANDOM THOUGHTS: So exactly whose signature adorns the magic letters of transit? Various scripts have it as either General de Gaulle or General Weygand. And thanks to actor Peter Lorre's heavy Hungarian accent—he had only learned English eight years earlier, just before coming to America—you can listen to this line over and over and still not figure it out.

Going on history, neither general makes sense as the signatory. We noted earlier that General de Gaulle, as the leader-in-exile of the Free France government, was in fact an enemy of the Vichy government. So his signature on a letter of transit would buy you trouble-a-plenty in Vichy-controlled Casablanca.

General Weygand was appointed head of the Allied forces during the Battle of France, when all signs already pointed to defeat. A miracle turnaround was not forthcoming, and he ended up recommending that France seek an armistice. After the June 1940 armistice he briefly served as the Vichy government's Minister of Defense, before being relegated to oversight duties for France in Africa.

But Hitler's distrust of Weygand ran deep. Hitler had not forgotten that at the end of World War I Weygand participated in the armistice-signing ceremony, and undertook for France a humiliating recitation of the armistice conditions. Convinced over time that Weygand was something less than a full collaborationist, Hitler forced his dismissal and retirement in November 1941. So in December 1941, when this scene is set, Weygand's signature on a letter of transit would not have been the answer either.

The real question here is, why use either name? These scenes were filmed two years after de Gaulle declared himself the leader of Free France, and several months after Hitler stripped Weygand of his powers, so it's not like there wasn't time to change the script. The simple solution here would have been to reference the Vichy government's head of state, Philippe Pétain.

EXPLANATION REQUIRED: Ugarte tells a waiter that he's expecting company and to bring over anyone who asks for him. Well, in a few minutes those people will be arriving, namely Victor Laszlo and Ilsa Lund. As Victor confirms later on **(30:13)**, he and Ugarte have plans to meet this evening. Victor and Ilsa are just as anxious to obtain those letters of transit as Ugarte is to unload them.

JUST WONDERING: Why does Ugarte think secreting the letters at Rick's is a good plan? It's one place the authorities are guaranteed to search—German officers are there every night after all. If his strategy is to hide the letters under the their noses, he'd be wise to reconsider. But perhaps subconsciously Ugarte knows his days are numbered, and this is, in a sense, his bequeathing of the letters to Rick.

CAST ANECDOTES: Playing the delightfully devious Ugarte is Peter Lorre. Lorre, who was Hungarian and Jewish, came to the United States in 1934; by the time *Casablanca* was made Lorre had established himself as top Hollywood portrayer of creepy bad guy types. The villainous bent to his career path can be traced directly to the 1931 German film classic *M*, in which he plays a deranged child murderer on the loose in Berlin. Through some haunting whistling and a hysterical plea for mercy that dwarfs in intensity Ugarte's upcoming plea to Rick for help, he is at his creepy best.

In fact, Lorre was too convincing in *M*—the German public thought he actually *was* that guy. This might have been manageable from a career standpoint, but when the Nazi propaganda machine began connecting Lorre's Jewish heritage to the loathsome characters he played, Lorre soon found himself in the hot seat.

So in February 1933, with the Nazi Party on the brink of absolute power and rumors afoot that Jews would soon be banned from German film (indeed two months later Germany's major film studio, UFA, did just that), Lorre said "Addio" to Berlin. Under cover of darkness he made his way to Vienna before ending up in the more Jewish-friendly confines of Paris.

As Lorre struggled to find work, British film director Alfred Hitchcock threw him a lifeline. Even though Lorre didn't know any English, Hitchcock thought he'd be perfect in the role of the sympathetic villain in *The Man Who Knew Too Much* (1934). Columbia Pictures took notice and, hungry for international talent, the studio extended Lorre a long-term deal before filming ever began. With that, in July 1934 Lorre and his new bride set out for Hollywood aboard the luxury liner *Majestic*, joining the initial wave of German émigrés to reach America after Hitler's rise to power.

JUST WONDERING: In the last shot of Bogart and Lorre standing face to face, is Bogart wearing lifts or is Lorre standing in a hole? **(12:25)** Bogart was 5' 8", three inches taller than Lorre. Yet, here it looks like Bogart has at least six inches on Lorre.

RANDOM THOUGHTS: Knowing that since 1933 the Nazis pretty well controlled the film industry, you would think foreign actors would avoid German pictures at all cost. This is particularly true given that scores of actors, including Lorre and Curt Bois, were fleeing the Berlin film scene out of fear for their safety. Well, apparently no one coached Ingrid Bergman on the matter. In April 1938, five years after the Nazis assumed power, and just weeks after Germany sacked Austria, Bergman agreed to make a picture in Berlin for Germany's premiere film studio. While the apolitical Bergman's desire to branch out from her Swedish film roots and increase her profile with Hollywood was understandable, this was not the most graceful way to do it.

FILM ANECDOTES: Rick and Ugarte's clandestine pact, including a good portion of the dialogue, comes directly from the play upon which the film is based, *Everybody Comes to Rick's*. This is just one of many scenes, plot devices and lines in the film that can be traced to the play. For example, the main plot device, the magical "letters of transit" that cannot be rescinded or questioned, is original to the play. And a host of scenes—Rick and Ugarte's talk, Rick and Renault's discussion in Rick's office, Strasser's casual but pointed grilling of Rick, Sam and Ilsa's exchange at the piano, Sam's counseling of Rick after hours, and Victor and Strasser's verbal showdown in Renault's office—are firmly rooted in the play.

That said, make no mistake—the play and the film differ dramatically, both in structure and content. In the play, the first night in the Café roughly tracks the film. But the next day things get bizarre in a hurry. It starts with the revelation that overnight Rick and Ilsa had a slumber party, thanks to Rick having slipped Ilsa his apartment key at the Café last night right under Victor and Renault's nose. Over breakfast the two giddily talk of skipping town, sans Victor of course. But Rick suddenly concludes that Ilsa only slept with him to obtain the letters of transit for her and Victor. In time, Victor shows up and Rick accuses him of orchestrating the scheme, calling him (ugh) a "high-class pimp."

Meanwhile, an overly amorous Renault becomes obsessed with the Bulgarian girl Annina, and when she spurns his visa-for-sex advances on the second night he turns her and her husband into fugitives. Rick hides the couple, and then brokers a deal with Renault for their safe passage out of Casablanca in exchange for coughing up Victor. The ending gambit unfolds largely as it does in the film, with one big exception, which we will tell you about when we get there.

Whatever the similarities, it's fair to say that the play probably would have had a short run on Broadway. The storyline is raw and the dialogue misses the mark throughout, with tawdry lines, hackneyed phrases from the era, and, for Sam's character, the unfortunate use of heavy racial dialect. Here are just a few examples of less-than-stellar dialogue:

> RICK TO UGARTE. You remind me of a pimp who's had a windfall. When he quits he's so sorry for the girls.
>
> RICK TO GERMAN PATRON. No dice, feller.
>
> YVONNE TO RICK. What a sucker I am...fall[ing] for a punk like you.
>
> RICK TO SAM. Play it, you dumb bastard.
>
> ILSA TO RICK. My heart did flip flops, Rick when you came down those stairs.
>
> SAM TO FERRARI. Thank yuh suh, but ah ain't got no time to spend what ah makes here.

Rick's—Main Room

MUSIC NOTES: Back in the main room, Sam launches into an audience participation song called "Knock on Wood," allowing patrons to commiserate about life in Casablanca. Everyone is having a grand time in the moment, but more than a few of Rick's patrons, including Ugarte, ought to be following the song's superstitious advice. Here's a sample verse sung by Sam:

> *Say, who's got trouble? We've got trouble.*
> *How much trouble? Too much trouble.*
> *Well now don't you frown, just knuckle down*
> *and knock on wood.*

The rest of the lyrics have Sam variously inquiring of the audience who's unhappy, who's unlucky, and who's got nothing, while assuring them that all these things can be solved simply by knocking on wood. In the film we hear all of the lyrics except for the bridge, which should have come between the "Who's got nothing?" and "Now who's happy?" verses. Overall the song is a nice thematic choice, given the down-and-out times most Café patrons are experiencing.

MUSIC NOTES: Of the many songs peppering *Casablanca*, "Knock on Wood" is the only one composed for the film. The song ended up being a last-minute replacement for a popular British wartime song called "Run Rabbit Run," which was being considered because it was featured in the original play. "Run Rabbit Run" too was an audience participation song, with patrons stomping their feet to simulate the chase. During World War II the Brits parodied the song with "Run Adolph Run."

Also slated for this scene was the jazz standard "Sweet Georgia Brown," which was to be played just before "Knock on Wood." The song was cut undoubtedly to tighten things up, and we say it was for the better.

CLOSER LOOK: In the first shot of the band playing "Knock on Wood" keep an eye on the drummer. He never hits the cymbal, though you can definitely hear one. Better yet, he's still going through the motions after the cymbal is no longer audible.

Now watch the piano keyboard and discover that Dooley Wilson isn't playing the notes. It's actually pretty funny to watch him just pat his way through the song as you hear the intricate ivory ticklings. Earlier, during "It Had to Be You" and "Shine," it's the same story; plus in "Shine" he also takes his right hand off the keyboard to swipe his head without the piano playing skipping a beat. **(7:18)**

All of Sam's piano work was dubbed for the very practical reason that Wilson didn't know how to play the piano. Rather, his instrument was the drums. The piano playing for Sam's songs is provided by piano man Elliot Carpenter, who played off-screen as the songs were filmed. Wilson did provide the smooth vocals, although producer Hal Wallis thought long and hard about dubbing those as well.

FILM ANECDOTES: Wallis struggled a bit with casting the role of the house piano player. In the play, the duties were performed by an African-American named Sam the Rabbit, and the character seemed like a natural one to carry over to the film. But several months before filming Wallis got stuck on the notion of recasting Sam as a woman, thinking specifically, among others, of Lena Horn and Ella Fitzgerald. After Wallis talked himself out of that idea, he brought Wilson in for a screen test. Wallis thought the test was "pretty good," but wasn't keen on Wilson's "flip, bouncy manner." He then fixated on veteran African-American character actor Clarence Muse. But when things didn't work out, he signed Wilson just a day or two before filming began, and that was that.

If you want to see more of Wilson in film, it's pretty slim pickings. In *Knock on Any Door* (1949), Bogart's first film venture after he left Warner Bros. to form his own production company, Wilson plays piano (barely) in a skid-row bar, with no lines and only thirty seconds of background screen-time, as Bogart's character chats up his gal. In *Two Tickets to London* (1943), a Michèle Morgan feature, Wilson tries his hand at the accordion.

JUST WONDERING: Couldn't Rick come up with a better place to hide the letters of transit than Sam's piano? Setting aside the fact that a Gestapo raid would root up those papers in no time, Rick secrets the papers at the very moment everyone's attention is focused on the spot where he is standing. Sure, he waits until the spotlight shines elsewhere, but it's not like it's pitch-black in the room. And even if he was convinced that the piano was the best place to hide the letters, why not wait until after-hours to secret them? Bottom line, Rick gets low marks here for this not-so-smooth move.

CLOSER LOOK: Note that the piano top opens up away from Sam, allowing Rick to slip the letters in from the far side. But that's not the way upright pianos typically open. Indeed, to facilitate a more surreptitious move the prop team actually reconfigured the piano top so it hinged the other way.

FILM ANECDOTES: For any Café scene, keep an eye trained on the background, where ominous shadows are cast on nearly every wall by an assortment of fronds, urns, screens and Moroccan-style lamps. In this scene, look for the huge shadow cast by a fretwork screen—there are a few of these in Rick's, including one fronting the host station. **(12:57)**

The heavy use of shadow is attributable to the film's producer. Wallis believed the film's success hinged on creating just the right mood in Rick's, and envisioned the Café as a dark, shadowy nook-of-a place; a natural host to a private rendezvous or illicit transaction.

Wallis complained throughout filming that the Café wasn't dark enough, and directed the head cinematographer to create "real black and whites" on the walls and background, and "dim, sketchy lighting." In the end the filming crew got it right, and was rewarded with an Academy Award nomination for Best Cinematography for a black-and-white film.

CLOSER LOOK: When Ferrari reaches his table he greets his friends by touching the fingers of his right hand first to his heart, then his mouth, and then his forehead. His friends respond in kind. The gesture is a variation on a traditional *salaam*, a greeting of peace consisting of a bow and a hand gesture to the forehead. It's common for the person arriving at a gathering to initiate a salaam, so Ferrari gets this part right.

RANDOM THOUGHTS: Apparently, when it comes to men's fashion in Casablanca, anything goes. Note that Ferrari is wearing a necktie *and* a cummerbund. Last time we checked, these two items do not a pair make. Probably just as well, though, as we can't picture Ferrari in a bow tie. And it could have been worse. The early versions of the wardrobe plot had Ferrari wearing "semi-native" attire. The rotund Greenstreet in harem pants? Now that would have been a sight.

MUSIC NOTES: During Rick and Ferrari's conversation Sam and his band play "The Very Thought of You." Written and composed by big band leader Ray Noble, this wildly popular song charted in 1934 not once but twice, with Noble's version hitting No. 1 and Bing Crosby's climbing to No. 11. It hit the charts again in 1944 when it appeared in a Warner Bros. film of the same name. The film is a likeable World War II romance that has an earnest new draftee taking a war bride, over objections from her dysfunctional family, in a mere forty-eight hours.

The song appears in *Casablanca* no doubt because it was in the Warner Bros. music library, meaning the studio could use it free of charge. Interestingly, the person calling the shots on popular songs liked this one enough to use it twice. "The Very Thought of You" can be heard the next night as well, as Carl and Sascha thank Rick for helping the Bulgarian couple win at roulette.

HISTORY LESSON: Rick refuses Ferrari's offers to buy the Café, remarking that Ferrari should let Rick run his own business. Ferrari replies that "isolationism" is not a practical approach in these times. This is one of the more obvious examples of the writers weaving in some topical political commentary. *Isolationism* is a foreign policy grounded in seclusion and avoiding the formation of alliances with other countries. The United States has a long history of dabbling in political isolationism, and the policy was never more popular than in the years leading up to World War II.

Churchill spent untold energy trying to convince America that standing on the sidelines while Hitler had his way abroad was a seriously flawed approach. His basic plea: Humanitarian and economic reasons abound compelling American intervention, and if Britain fell Hitler would be knocking on America's door soon after.

But there's a certain cold logic to isolationism's premise—keeping your nose out of the affairs of others. And that logic rang true with many Americans, particularly after the massive casualties seen in World War I. The most vocal and powerful isolationist group was the America First Committee, whose principal spokesperson was aviation legend Charles Lindbergh. While some non-interventionist groups were okay with certain aid to Europe, Lindbergh and his followers believed Europe should fend for itself.

Roosevelt took numerous steps to aid Britain and its allies and get America more involved in the war. But, feeling the political constraints of Congress and public opinion, he always stopped short of belligerency. In the end, only Pearl Harbor silenced the isolationists. Just a few days after the attack the America First Committee disbanded. As payback for Lindbergh's outspokenness, Roosevelt saw to it that America's most acclaimed flier did not serve in uniform during the war.

RANDOM THOUGHTS: Little does Rick know, but just *five days* from now America will find itself at war..1ye and ear out for a rare voice dubbing in this scene. As Rick escorts Yvonne out of the Café she snaps at Rick for pushing her around. But watch her lips and it's clear that Yvonne is not saying the words.

So what is she saying? Hard to tell, but pre-production the script had the following additional line: "...I'm a lady. I played the Palace. I've been married twice." From these remarks we surmise that Yvonne is a well-regarded French chanteuse. Makes perfect sense, given the très chic outfits she wears to the Café and her singing stint later in the film.

RANDOM THOUGHTS: Earlier we revealed one of two *Casablanca* cast marriages. The second one was between Madeleine LeBeau (Yvonne) and Marcel Dalio (Emil the croupier). But by the time filming started they were in divorce mode. Talk about your May-December relationships. When they first dated Dalio was a creaky forty, while LeBeau was a mere fifteen and-a-half. At least they had enough sense to wait until LeBeau turned sixteen to get married.

CAST ANECDOTES: How Dalio and LeBeau got from Paris to Hollywood is a wild story and well worth the long version. In the late spring of 1940, with the Germans bearing down on Paris, Dalio suddenly realized that his Jewish heritage, combined with his celebrity status, made him a marked man. Dalio wisely fled Paris with LeBeau for the French city of Biarritz, located near the France-Spain border. Unable to secure American visas, the couple finagled two for Chile. Dalio then obtained coveted French exit visas by bribing a French official with his car. As Dalio later explained, what good would the car do him in Auschwitz?

Finally in Lisbon, they gained passage on a Chilean-bound ship called the *Quanza*. Before leaving they learned that the ship would be making a stop in Mexico, so they hustled up temporary visas for that country as well.

In late August the ship made port in New York. *The New York Times* noted matter-of-factly that a "French film actor" named Marcel Dalio was aboard, along with six American ambulance drivers captured and released by the Germans, a Japanese journalist, a Czechoslovakian figure skater, the editor of the Parisian newspaper *Paris-Soir*, a Paris opera singer and "lowly refugees from virtually all the countries Hitler has conquered." The newspaper failed to mention, however, that only passengers with American visas were allowed to disembark; that group did not include Dalio and LeBeau.

With Dalio, LeBeau and eighty others still aboard, the *Quanza* headed off to Veracruz, Mexico. But Mexican officials would not allow entry even to those carrying Mexican visas, insisting that the visas had been issued without authorization. A frustrated captain decided to forgo Chile and head back to Europe. The refugees viewed this development as a virtual death sentence.

On the way back the *Quanza* ported in Norfolk, Virginia. By that time Dalio and others had contacted various American lawyers and refugee organizations, in hopes of gaining entry on this second go-around. One Jewish refugee organization asked First Lady Eleanor Roosevelt to appeal to the president himself. It worked, and over the protestations of his own Secretary of State, President Roosevelt saw to it that all of the *Quanza's* remaining passengers were granted temporary entry visas.

Once on American soil Dalio was determined to stay. Still, as political refugees he and LeBeau had a mere thirty days before they would be sent on to Chile. From New York, Dalio networked with other exiled Frenchmen to find an acting job in Montreal, Canada. Once there, he quickly obtained American visas, and skipped town by plane back to New York. One cross-country train trip later he and LeBeau arrived in Los Angeles, knowing no English and with seventeen dollars to their names.

CAST ANECDOTES: Although Dalio and LeBeau never share a scene together in *Casablanca*, they do share scenes in their only other film together, *Paris After Dark* (1943). It's an entertaining wartime melodrama about the psyche of the French citizenry at the height of the Nazi occupation of Paris. Dalio plays a slick-talking French barber and Nazi turncoat who can't resist hitting on LeBeau's French barmaid character.

Their scenes together are priceless. As LeBeau's character spurns Dalio's advances, even cooling him off with a glass of water to the face, you can't help but think they took hidden pleasure acting these scenes in light of their recent and less-than-amicable divorce.

Added bonuses here are LeBeau singing a soulful French tune that leaves everyone with a lump in their throat just as "La Marseillaise" does in *Casablanca*, and the appearance of another *Casablanca* actor, Curt Bois, as a high-spirited, in-the-trenches member of the French Resistance.

Rick's—Terrace

CLOSER LOOK: Just as Rick lights up a much-needed smoke, he is himself lit up by the blinding light of the airport's beacon. An awfully tight spotlight, we say, given that the beacon is perched atop the control tower, which is several hundred yards off. Anyway, the brief shot included here of the tower actually is a scaled model. A respectable rendering to be sure, but the main giveaway is that there was no beacon atop the real control tower. This is verified in the earlier airport tarmac scene. **(5:18)**

The beacon-inspired lighting effects pop up in other scenes, including shots outside the Café's main entrance at the beginning and end of the first night, shots inside the Café before and after Rick's Paris flashback and in Rick's apartment on the second night after Rick and Ilsa settle their differences.

FILM ANECDOTES: Earlier we mentioned a connection we discovered between *Casablanca* and another Warner Bros. film, *Background to Danger* (1943), and this scene contains that connection. While we were screening the film for the antics of Greenstreet and Lorre we noticed a familiar sight. At the end of the film there's a shot of a plane taking off, with hangars visible in the background. And wouldn't you know it, it's the exact same shot used here for the Casablanca Airport.

Recycling this shot in *Background to Danger* makes perfect sense given that Warner Bros. cranked out the film just a few months after *Casablanca*, and the studio was always looking for ways to trim production costs.

But wait, we have yet another Warner Bros. film for you that recycles an airport clip from *Casablanca*. *One More Tomorrow* (1946) depicts LaGuardia Airport by using the exact same close up of the tower, with the beacon circling, seen here in *Casablanca*. And as a bonus, the airplane shown on the runway in *One More Tomorrow* matches up perfectly with the model plane used in *Casablanca*. Now, *One More Tomorrow* was released in 1946, but it was actually filmed during the first half of 1943, which makes the airplane model reuse all the more likely.

CLOSER LOOK: Earlier the film hinted that Rick's Café was near the airport when Strasser's plane passed over a sign for the Café as it came in for a landing. Well, the shot here of Rick and Renault watching a plane take off from the airport definitively places the Café, not just near the airport, but right at the end of the runway. From the Café's terrace, Rick and Renault have an unobstructed view of the same hangars we saw in the earlier airport scenes.

The Café's proximity to the airport does hold up in the broader context, but barely. It means that when Strasser and Renault discussed the Café at the airport, Renault could have just pointed to it at the end of the runway. It also means that at film's end, Rick, Renault, Victor and Ilsa only drive a few hundred yards from the Café to the airport.

EXPLANATION REQUIRED: Round two of Casselle and Tonelli's three-round verbal spar takes place here on the terrace. In French, Casselle chides Tonelli over Italy's invasion of little Greece, calling the invasion cowardly and accusing the Italian army of not being able to win without Germany's help. Here's the translation:

> Me, I tell you the attitude of Italy is disgusting!
> What would you have done without the German army?
> It's incredible! That poor little country, it corresponds, my friend, to nothing.
> After you. (opening the door for Tonelli)

HISTORY LESSON: Casselle pretty much hit the mark here in his assessment of the Italian military. Here's the background on Italy's "conquest" of Greece. Looking for the quick military kill, Italy invaded neighboring Greece on October 28, 1940. Italy launched the attack from neighboring Albania, which it had overrun the previous year. But the Italians got far more than they bargained for from the Greek army. Not only did the plucky Greeks fend off the Italians, they boldly launched a counterattack and in a matter of months had taken a good chunk of Albania.

A full five months later the Italians were still floundering, and in the process had exposed Germany to an Allied attack from the south. By April 1941 Hitler had seen enough, and ordered his own invasion of Greece. After a few hard-fought weeks of battle, Greece finally fell to Axis forces.

RANDOM THOUGHTS: When Rick and Renault share a laugh over Casselle and Tonelli's argument, it's the rare smile that Rick cracks during his time in Casablanca. In the Paris flashback, of course, he is all smiles while drinking champagne in his apartment and at La Belle Aurore. But in Casablanca, there's not much for him to smile about. Look for glimpses of smiles when he passes Sam playing "Baby Face," when he mocks Renault for being a German toady and when he listens to Emil the croupier gripe about Jan winning at roulette. And near the end of the film, a small chuckle in Renault's office. But that's about it.

CLOSER LOOK: Some continuity problems pop up in this scene involving Rick and his smoking habit. After kicking Yvonne to the curb, Rick starts to light up. But when the shot cuts to Rick joining Renault, he's nearly finished with the smoke. A few seconds later Rick moves to light up another one, then pauses when he hears a plane taking off from the airport. But when the shot changes to show the plane, Rick's cigarette is now lit. All of this goes to show that trying to retain scene continuity when cigarettes are in the mix is not an easy task.

DID YOU KNOW?: As Rick and Renault watch another plane take off for Lisbon, Renault asks Rick if he'd like to be on it. Rick asks blankly why he would ever want to go to Lisbon, which prompts Renault to point out that the Clipper to America is there. This is a real-world reference that anyone watching the film back in 1943 would have understood. The Clipper refers to a fleet of seaplanes built by Pan American Airways in the late 1930s. In June 1939, a Pan Am Clipper made the first trans-Atlantic passenger flight.

Pan Am mapped two main routes across the Atlantic, a northern one from New York to England via Newfoundland, and a southern one from New York to Marseille, France via Bermuda, the Azores and Lisbon, Portugal. Total flight time to Lisbon was some twenty-nine hours, as long as rough weather or the obligatory mechanical breakdown didn't strand you for a spell in Bermuda or the Azores.

All in all, the accommodations were pretty nice, with sleeping, dining and lounge quarters spread out over two levels and spacious enough to accommodate forty passengers on overnight hauls. Indeed, when President Roosevelt traveled to the Casablanca Conference in January 1943 he did so in relative comfort aboard a Clipper.

RANDOM THOUGHTS: On the continuity front, the timing of Captain Renault's Clipper reference checks out. With the onset of the war in September 1939, Pan Am abandoned the northern route. But the United States allowed the airline to continue service to Lisbon (but not Marseille) via the southern route. The Clipper then became a lifeline to America for stranded Americans and Europeans who were lucky enough to get to Lisbon *and* could afford the rather pricey ticket. For the common folk, the more likely mode of transportation was steerage aboard a passenger ship; and rest assured there was price gouging aplenty.

DID YOU KNOW?: While civilian flights in and out of Lisbon were relatively safe, owing to both sides respecting the neutrality of Portugal and Spain, they were by no means risk-free. Indeed, in June 1943 British stage and film great Leslie Howard lost his life on a flight from Lisbon to England when German fighters intercepted and strafed his plane over the Bay of Biscay; all seventeen aboard died.

Theories abound as to why the Germans downed the plane. German pilots involved in the incident insisted they simply mistook the plane for an enemy aircraft. Others believe something nefarious was afoot. One theory is that it was an assassination attempt on Winston Churchill, with German agents mistaking Howard's rotund, cigar-smoking traveling companion for Churchill. Another is that the Germans targeted Howard either as a spy or as payback for his ongoing anti-Nazi efforts.

To be sure the Nazis despised him, and just the year before Howard had poked them in the eye with the powerful anti-Nazi film *Pimpernel Smith* (1942), in which his character rescues intellectuals and other sorts from the clutches of the Third Reich. *Der Angriff*, the infamous Nazi propaganda magazine that was referenced just a few scenes ago, reportedly boasted something to the effect of *Pimpernel Smith Has Made His Last Trip*.

Perhaps best known for his role as Ashley in *Gone with the Wind* (1939), Howard's performances with Bergman in *Intermezzo: A Love Story* (1939) and Bogart in *The Petrified Forest* (1936) are must-sees.

CAST ANECDOTES: Perhaps no one in Hollywood was more saddened by the loss of Leslie Howard than Humphrey Bogart. The two were long-time friends and Bogart, it can be fairly said, owed his film career to Howard. In 1935, Bogart landed the role second to Howard's lead in the Broadway play *The Petrified Forest*. The role of Duke Mantee, an escaped convict who takes Howard and others hostage in an Arizona roadside Bar-B-Q restaurant, seemingly was made for Bogart's gruff, hard-hearted acting persona. The stage chemistry between Bogart and Howard was unmistakable, and the reviews read accordingly.

So intrigued by the play was Jack Warner that he hopped a train to New York to see it. A few days later, Warner secured the film rights to the work from Howard and his partners. At the same time, Howard convinced Warner to retain Bogart as Mantee. But as filming neared Warner Bros. changed course, announcing that its leading gangster heavy, Edward G. Robinson, would assume the role. A devastated Bogart appealed to Howard, and Howard stepped up. Shortly before shooting began Howard invoked his heavyweight status, and fired off a telegram to Warner with the following assured words: INSIST BOGART PLAY MANTEE NO BOGART NO DEAL. Warner backed down and Howard and Bogart were reunited on screen, again to rave reviews.

It seemed improbable that the rough-edged Bogart would hit it off with a British-gentleman type. But so it was, with their experience working together on *The Petrified Forest* developing into a life-long bond. Indeed Bogart's connection to Howard ran so deep that in 1952, nine years after Howard's death, Bogart was moved to name his newborn daughter Leslie Howard Bogart.

RANDOM THOUGHTS: Rick, in full wise guy mode, tells Renault that he moved to Casablanca for the waters. Renault questions him, noting wryly that Casablanca is in the desert. Well, that's not at all true. Casablanca, as we now know, a port city on the Atlantic Ocean and, while it ain't exactly raining buckets there, it's not dry enough to qualify as desert. If Renault wants to experience true desert, say, something less than ten inches of rainfall a year, he needs to head south of Casablanca or, even better, east to the Saharan sand dunes on the other side of the Atlas Mountains. So on this geographic point it is Renault who is misinformed.

RANDOM THOUGHTS: So far Rick seems like a well-principled guy, so it would be a shock to discover that he's running a dishonest gambling establishment, right? But we get our first hint that not all games are on the level when Emil the croupier approaches Rick on the terrace, clearly upset over the house having just lost 20,000 francs. His concern is not all that surprising, but it is odd that Emil feels personally responsible. And when Emil later promises Rick there will be no more payouts like that one, suspicions are raised. So is the roulette table at Rick's on the up-and-up? Stay tuned.

Rick's—Main Room

MUSIC NOTES: As Rick and Renault weave through the Café, Sam plays the standard "Baby Face." As with many of the popular songs used in the film, this one topped the charts in 1926, the same year it was penned. In 1933 Warner Bros. used the song for a film of the same name. Now given the light, innocent nature of the song, you would think the film's content would follow suit. But Warner Bros. went the opposite direction. The scandalous storyline features a speakeasy waitress with harlot-esque qualities who heads to Manhattan and sleeps her way through the corporate ranks, all in the name of baubles. This picture was made just before Hollywood entered its notorious censorship era, and many credit it for accelerating the era's onset. Why was it used in *Casablanca*? In the absence of any real thematic fit, the practical answer is that, once again, the price was right—"Baby Face" was in the Warner Bros. song library.

CLOSER LOOK: Walking past Sam, Renault gives Rick the heads up that he'll be arresting a murderer in the Café tonight, then warns Rick not to tip off the suspect. But Renault never actually tells Rick the name of the suspect he's not supposed to tip off. No matter. It's clear from Rick's earlier exchange with Ugarte that he knows of whom Renault speaks.

DID YOU KNOW?: In response to Renault's warning, Rick says he sticks his neck out for nobody. Renault sees this as "wise foreign policy." This comment picks up on the isolationist theme introduced earlier in the evening. It goes without saying that Rick is meant to personify the United States and its politics, and Rick's refusal to stick his neck out pretty well sums up the United States' initial outlook on the war.

EXPLANATION REQUIRED: In the third and final round of Casselle and Tonelli's running feud, Casselle, speaking in French, asks Tonelli, "You and Corsica, Tunisia, Nice—what did you do to get them?" At the time all three were controlled by France's Vichy government. So what is this discussion all about? Well, Italy believed it was the rightful owner of these lands and wanted them back, and it seems that Casselle is mocking Italy's stance on the matter.

Here's the history underlying this squabble. Italian dictator Benito Mussolini subscribed to a political doctrine known as *irredentism*, whereby a country justifies sacking lands based on either prior ownership or close cultural or historical ties. Before the war he had mostly just talked about it. But when Hitler reduced it to practice with his invasion of Austria, Mussolini realized he'd better make his own reclamation plans known, else be shut out on the spoils of war.

On November 30, 1938, Italy's Minister of Foreign Affairs gave a Mussolini-endorsed speech to Italy's Fascist Party leaders, the purpose of which was to fire up the political base on expanding Italy's holdings. The speech was met with chants of "Tunis, Corsica, Nice, Savoy!" and led to demonstrations in the streets of Rome. The media reported the events the next day, setting the wheels in motion for the "return" of these lands to Italy.

HISTORY LESSON: So did Italy have any legitimate claim to Nice, Corsica or Tunisia? Well, it's complicated.

Nice. In 1860, the kingdom of Sardinia agreed to cede Nice to France as payment for France supporting Sardinia's war with Austria and its efforts to create a unified Italy. A year later, modern day Italy was born by merging Sardinia-controlled regions, sans Nice, with ones in the Italian peninsula. It no doubt hurt to see Nice slip away at the last minute, but Lieutenant Casselle would argue that this was a Sardinia-sanctioned deal, not a France land grab.

Corsica. For centuries this Mediterranean island was controlled by the republic of Genoa, which became part of unified Italy. In 1768, Genoa sought French military aid to quell some local uprisings. Unable to repay France for its services, Genoa granted France administrative rights over the island until it could make good on the debt. With its foot in the door, France eventually annexed the island. France's military power play here gives Italy and Captain Tonelli more to complain about.

Tunisia. Italy had its eyes on Tunisia shortly after its 1861 unification. It's just across the Mediterranean Sea from Italy and shares a border with Libya, which was already under Italian control. In 1869, Tunisia was in financial distress. Great Britain, France and Italy eagerly jumped in to help, each hoping to induce colonization through financial dependence. For years, Italy took the lead on economic aid and colonization efforts. But in 1881 France claimed that Tunisia had encroached on Algerian lands and used that as an excuse to move troops into Tunisia. France soon had another protectorate. While France was the aggressor here as well, there's room for Lieutenant Casselle to say that Italy misplayed its hand—it had plenty of opportunities to seize Tunisia, and should have realized that France would eventually pounce.

CHAPTER 3

THE GAME CONTINUES

"I stick my neck out for nobody."
— Rick

Pressing house business sends Rick and Captain Renault in from the terrace and up to Rick's office. Along the way Renault shares with Rick three interesting items. First, there will be an arrest in the Café tonight, of a murderer no less, and there's little doubt Ugarte's the target. Second, Major Strasser will be in attendance this evening, in part to take in the arrest escapades.

Third, a war celebrity of sorts has surfaced in Casablanca. Victor Laszlo, renowned leader of the Czech Resistance, has endured untold torture at the hands of the Germans and defied all odds by escaping from a German concentration camp and making his way south to Morocco. But Victor wants to make his stay a short one. According to Renault, Victor is combing the black market for two exit visas. Renault admonishes Rick not to assist Victor in his efforts to skip town. Renault, you see, is wise to the fact that Rick has come to the aid of more than a few underdogs over the years.

News of Strasser's arrival sends Renault hustling downstairs to set the stage for Ugarte's arrest. On Renault's instructions, a team of gendarmes approach Ugarte in the gambling room. Ugarte seems to realize he's done for. Still, his slippery instincts kick in and he makes a run for it. Ugarte exchanges gunfire with the gendarmes, and in retreat begs Rick for help. But Rick is unwilling to stick his neck out any further, and Ugarte is quickly cornered and nabbed. An embarrassed Rick apologizes to his patrons for the unseemly disturbance, and coolly urges them to resume their good time.

Thankfully, the rest of the night is less eventful, and has Strasser, Renault, Rick, Sam, Victor and his companion, Ms. Ilsa Lund, playing a lively game of musical chairs. The game kicks off with Renault waving Rick over to Strasser's table. Strasser and another German officer quiz Rick, and in the process convey that they have their eye on Rick and will not tolerate anyone helping Victor leave Casablanca. Rick tells them what they want to hear, that he's a neutral sort and not inclined to get involved.

Seconds later Victor and Ilsa enter the Café. The two are on a mission to find Ugarte and the letters of transit. Just after they sit down a man approaches their table, ostensibly to hock a ring. At once the man reveals he's a fellow member of the Resistance. But before anything goes down the clandestine exchange is cut short by a visit from Renault.

The ever-cordial Renault welcomes Victor and Ilsa to Casablanca and extends genuine compliments to both. Ilsa quickly changes subjects, asking about the house piano player she saw as they entered the Café. Renault explains that Sam followed the Café's owner, Rick, from Paris. From her questions and body language we get the impression she knows them.

Soon Renault waves Strasser over to the table for introductions. In contrast to Renault's hospitable tone, Strasser's visit is tension-filled. Strasser makes clear to Victor that he's in his crosshairs, and Victor lets Strasser know that he's up to the challenge. Seeking to keep the heat on, Strasser presses for a meeting with Victor in Renault's office tomorrow morning.

With that confrontation behind him, Victor sets out to revisit his talk with the ring purveyor. At the bar he learns some disheartening news: Ugarte will not be able to deliver the exit visas as planned. Meanwhile, Ilsa gains Sam's attention. We now know for sure that Sam, Rick and Ilsa know each other from bygone days. Ilsa asks Sam to play an old favorite for her. Ordinarily not a problem, except that Rick has apparently forbidden Sam to play the particular song requested, and he is none too happy to be hearing it upon his return to the main room. Like a shot, Rick heads over to Sam, where he gets two unwelcome, heart-skipping surprises: Ilsa, his former lover is in the house, and she's here with one Victor Laszlo.

Rick has no choice but to play it cool and join the party (Renault included) for the final, and rather awkward, table gathering of the night. Mainly this exchange has Rick and Ilsa acknowledging their prior acquaintance and conversing in a not-so-clever-double-entendre sort of way that practically shouts, "We have history!" Their exchange leaves Renault jealous and Victor wondering what the heck is going on here.

On the way out the door Victor invites Ilsa to explain who this Rick character is. Ilsa's reply? She's not sure...but she did see him a lot in Paris. And with that confession of sorts we strongly suspect there will be romantic troubles ahead for these three.

Rick's—Rick's Office

HISTORY LESSON: Renault refers to tonight's important guest as Major Strasser of the Third Reich. So what exactly is the Third Reich, and for that matter what about the First and Second Reichs? Well, it's fairly straightforward once armed with the knowledge that *reich* means empire.

The First Reich refers to the Holy Roman Empire, which doesn't sound particularly German in nature, but was in fact an ever-shifting collection of European lands that centered around Germanic states. It began in the 9th or 10th century (depending on your source) and wrapped up in 1806 thanks to Napoleon's successes during the early years of the Napoleonic Wars.

The Second Reich, going by the more straightforward name of the German Empire, began in 1871 when a recently formed and Prussia-dominated confederation of northern German states forged a unified Germany by bringing southern German states, sans Austria, into the fold. It ended in 1918 with Germany's defeat in World War I.

The Third Reich was Hitler's vision of a rather more expansive German empire, with the likes of Poland, Austria, Czechoslovakia, the Netherlands, France and Belgium being the early supplements. He boldly proclaimed that this third iteration would last 1,000 years. Not quite.

CLOSER LOOK: Confirmed during the exchange is the fact that Rick lets Renault win at roulette. Smart move on Rick's part to keep the police chief's pockets lined. Rick's ability to control goings-on at the roulette table will take on greater significance tomorrow night.

RANDOM THOUGHTS: Impressed by Victor's resourcefulness when it comes to outfoxing the Third Reich, Rick bets Renault 10,000 francs that Victor will make it out of Casablanca. 10,000 francs would be worth around $250 U.S. dollars. A $250 bet made in 1941 is equivalent to a $4,250 bet made today, so the stakes are high here.

DID YOU KNOW?: During the chat Renault discloses two intriguing facts from Rick's past that actually coincide with real-world events. In 1935 Rick ran guns to Ethiopia, which is a reference to the Second Italo-Ethiopian War of 1935-36. In 1936 Rick fought in the Spanish Civil War on the Loyalist side. Rick clearly has an anti-fascist streak in him—both fights had Rick working to defeat fascist incursions.

HISTORY LESSON: Here's the story behind Rick's days as a war volunteer supporting Ethiopia in its fight against Italy's infamous fascist dictator, Benito Mussolini. Il Duce had his sights set on Ethiopia for some time, seeking retribution for the humiliating defeat Italy suffered at the hands of its former East-African colony some four decades earlier. A border skirmish in late 1934 opened the door, and by October of the next year Mussolini had ordered an all-out invasion.

The United States declared itself neutral in the war, and imposed embargoes on both countries. For a time Britain and France actually imposed arms embargoes on Ethiopia, but not Italy. In America, Ethiopia garnered slivers of support from communist organizations fighting fascism as well as from African-American communities hoping to save from empirical defeat Africa's lone independently run country. In Harlem, men drilled in preparation for joining the war. In Chicago protesters marched to the cry "Hands Off Ethiopia." Two industrious African-American pilots even flew to Ethiopia to command Ethiopia's meager air force. But in the end foreign volunteer support for Ethiopia was limited. While Ethiopia managed to hang on until August 1936, Italy's arsenal, which inexcusably included a heavy dose of chemical weapons, proved too much.

HISTORY LESSON: Rick's involvement in the Spanish Civil War is no less intriguing. This war pitted the left-leaning Republican government, known as the Loyalists, against the fascist-based Nationalist rebels. The Nationalists had the full backing of Hitler, so choosing sides in this one was not difficult either. Loyalist backers from around the world descended on Spain, forming the International Brigade; some 2,800 of these volunteers were Americans.

Rick likely would have been a member of the Abraham Lincoln Brigade. If he arrived in the first wave he would have landed in Spain in February 1937, only to be thrown into a virtual suicide mission on the front at Jarama, just outside Madrid. Rick's efforts notwithstanding, after three years of bloodshed the Nationalists prevailed, kicking off a thirty-six-year dictatorship for General Francisco Franco.

CLOSER LOOK: Renault appears to be well-decorated, with three medals prominently displayed on his left chest. We got to wondering whether they are real French medals. In this scene, a close up of Renault allows us to confirm that they are either authentic or pretty darn good replicas. Here's the story behind each one.

The medal on your right is France's commemorative medal from *La Grande Guerre*, that is, The Great War. **(19:20)** The medal's ribbon is red-and-white striped. Its front features the profile of a female figure (representing France) wearing a French military helmet and holding a sword. Renault received this medal for his service in World War I.

The one in the middle is the French version of the Inter-Allied Victory Medal from World War I. Each Allied country designed its own victory medal, with variations on two common themes—a double-rainbow striped ribbon, and a depiction of Nike, the winged Greek goddess of victory. The French version featured Nike's outstretched arms, visible on Renault's medal. Again, Renault earned this one simply by serving in World War I.

The medal on your left is quite impressive. It's the badge of France's Legion of Honor, a civil and military order of merit established by Napoleon I. We like to think Renault earned his for some act of gallantry on the battlefield. The medal is a five-sided double-pointed star, suspended from a red ribbon, with a wreath in between. From this particular design we know that Renault is a Chevalier or Knight, the introductory class of the five Legion of Honor classes. If he's looking to move up the Legion ranks he'd better pick the right side in this war.

CAST ANECDOTES: Bogart himself received the United States' version of the Inter-Allied Victory Medal for his service in the U.S. Navy in the last months of the war. He nearly *didn't* receive it, though, when he missed his ship while on leave and was promptly declared a deserter. He did serve a few days in confinement for his mistake, but eventually the medal and an honorable discharge came his way.

EXPLANATION REQUIRED: When Renault says he has orders to keep Victor in Casablanca, Rick responds "I see, Gestapo spank," inferring Renault is under the German thumb. The term is a holdover from the original play. No insight on its origin is available beyond that, but in the play Renault replies that Rick's use of the term makes him sound like an American reporter.

RANDOM THOUGHTS: During his arguments with Captain Tonelli, Lieutenant Casselle speaks with a heavy French accent. But here, when advising Renault in English that Strasser is in the Café, the accent disappears and Casselle sounds more American than French.

Rick's—Main Room

RANDOM THOUGHTS: Somebody better tell Renault that he left his gloves in Rick's office. They're in Renault's hand when Rick retrieves money from the safe **(18:22)**, but by the time he sits on the couch, they've disappeared. We suggest looking over by the brandy decanter.

CLOSER LOOK: Check out the wild cocktail Carl is set to deliver. **(20:46)** Any drink featuring an orange peel spiral is sure to boost war-beleaguered spirits. The drink also shows up the next night, imbibed by the French officer who gives Yvonne a hard time at the bar. **(1:02:38)** Our best guess is it's a Gin Cooler, a popular drink in the early 1940s.

MUSIC NOTES: As Renault and his team prepare to nab Ugarte, the band rolls out yet another classic, "I'm Just Wild About Harry." This tune was penned for the 1921 Broadway musical hit *Shuffle Along* by the renowned African-American composition team of Eubie Blake and Noble Sissle. It's a light love song, so it doesn't much tie in to what's happening on-screen, other than the fact that the gendarmes are wild about nabbing Ugarte. For a nice singing rendition of this song (plus "It Had to Be You") in another Bogart film, check out *The Roaring Twenties* (1939).

DID YOU KNOW?: Strasser and his toady, Herr Heinz, may be barbarians, but they certainly have refined tastes: it's champagne and caviar for them both. In a show of hospitality, Renault recommends to Strasser a bottle of 1926 Veuve Clicquot champagne.

So does Renault know his champagnes? We contacted the folks at Veuve Clicquot Ponsardin to see what kind of year 1926 was for the house. Turns out this really was an exceptional year. Here are the details.

Early in the 1926 growing season, rain, hail, something called chlorosis, and some hungry caterpillars combined to wipe out a full seventy-five percent of the grapes. But the grapes that survived nature's wrath enjoyed near-perfect late-season weather, and were of such good quality that 1926 was deemed a "vintage" year—a distinction bestowed upon only the best years. So who knew Captain Renault was an oenophile?

As for Veuve Clicquot Ponsardin, the house has been making champagne in Reims, France since 1772. It has survived two world wars—in the first one, the Germans basically used Reims, and all its champagne houses, as target practice for four years. Much of the house's storied history revolves around its matriarch, Madame Clicquot, affectionately known as the Grande Dame of Champagne. Madame Clicquot was a tough old bird if there ever was one, with a nose for business. She inherited the family business in 1805 after being widowed at the age of twenty-seven;

An actual bottle of 1926 vintage Veuve Clicquot.

and wouldn't you know it, that's where the house name comes from—*veuve* in French means *widow*. Among her grand accomplishments, Madame Clicquot is credited with hitting upon a process called *riddling*, which solved the, um, riddle of how to eliminate unsightly sediment from champagne.

RANDOM THOUGHTS: If you're thinking that it would be nice to throw a *Casablanca* party and break out a bottle of 1926 Veuve Clicquot in themed celebration, you can pretty well forget it. Beneath the house, locked in the far reaches of the labyrinth of chalk caves, rest the last few bottles of the 1926 vintage. The bottles, all magnums, are stored in darkness and upside-down in A-frame wine racks called *pupitres*. The labels are well worn, but the house assures us that the contents remain eminently drinkable. And, the house adds, they are not for sale.

FILM ANECDOTES: Just before filming, the script had Strasser returning Renault's favor by providing a wine recommendation of his own. Renault was to order a glass of Rhine wine in deference to his German guests. Strasser then was to suggest that Renault try instead a wine from Reutlingen, Germany, a town just south of Stuttgart. A decent-enough parallel exchange, but apparently someone thought it was too long to travel for the limited payoff, and it got halved.

JUST WONDERING: What other intriguing tidbits does the Rick Blaine dossier include? As Strasser takes the dossier back from Rick you can see handwriting on an exposed page. **(24:30)** Unfortunately, none of it's legible. This is one prop from the film that doesn't receive much attention, but it sure would be great to have and to see those scribblings.

Rick's—Gambling Room

RANDOM THOUGHTS: It's a little odd that the gendarmes are so polite to Ugarte, who is after all a murder suspect. We thought Renault wanted to make a big splash for Strasser. Yet his men approach Ugarte in the gambling room and matter-of-factly ask him to join them, with no handcuffs or strong-arming. Heck, they even accommodate Ugarte's thinly-veiled stall tactic—a request to first cash in his chips. But that's good news for us, as it sets the stage for Ugarte's entertaining, against-all-odds escape attempt.

MUSIC NOTES: Notice that, because the band is playing in the main room and Ugarte is hanging out in the gambling room, you can't hear "I'm Just Wild About Harry" playing in the gambling room until the gendarmes open the doors connecting the two rooms. A nice attention to detail by the sound crew.

EXPLANATION REQUIRED: As Ugarte gets the hook, the croupier shouts various table instructions in French:

- The game continues!
- The incident is closed, Madame.
- Place your bets, gentlemen, ladies!
- Mark your bets—the game continues!
- The bets are made. Lay your bets!

On its face this is your standard croupier banter. But you can't help but think that the line *the game continues* has some deeper meaning here. Life in Casablanca appears to be one big game of survival—people come and go, and the game rolls on.

CLOSER LOOK: Ugarte has somehow managed to misplace his hat. When he visited Rick at his table earlier, he had a bowler hat in hand. **(10:16)**

RANDOM THOUGHTS: During his escape bid, with a cigarette still dangling from his mouth, Ugarte fires four shots at the charging gendarmes. His targets are just a few feet away and yet Ugarte manages to miss them all. Further evidence, perhaps, that Ugarte wasn't the triggerman for the German couriers after all. Anyway, look for Abdul reacting to the first two shots as if one caught him in the shoulder. We do see him a few scenes later, so apparently it was just a flesh wound.

Rick's—Main Room

RANDOM THOUGHTS: A continuity gaffe occurs when the crowd in the main room reacts to the source of the commotion surrounding Ugarte's arrest. Other scenes have the gambling room off the left side of the main room, when facing the bar. But here the crowd reacts to noise coming from the *opposite* side of the room. **(22:15)** Indeed, in the next scene things are back to normal when Ugarte races out around the corner near the bar, meaning he entered and crossed the main room from the left.

JUST WONDERING: Responding to a patron's insinuation that he left Ugarte hanging out to dry, Rick says he sticks his neck out for nobody. Has he forgotten that earlier in the evening he stuck his neck out for Ugarte in a huge way by agreeing to secret the letters of transit? Let's hope Captain Renault and his men overlook the piano when they give the Café a good ransacking, or Rick and his extended neck will have some explaining to do.

CLOSER LOOK: Earlier we mentioned our hunch that the same actor plays two patrons in Rick's. Look for the woman Rick passes by just after his "stick my neck out" line. That sure looks like the woman Rick just waved into the gambling room. Hopefully she got paid for both roles.

MUSIC NOTES: Looking to restore order in the wake of Ugarte's arrest, Rick instructs Sam to resume playing. Sam's choice is a catchy ballad, "Heaven Can Wait," which topped the charts in 1939. It's a suitably soothing song for Rick's patrons, but not so much for Ugarte—in just a few more hours his wait for heaven will be over.

This song was a late substitution for two other songs considered for the slot. Early on the production team penciled in "Old Man Moses," which had been used in the original play. But it's a dirge-like sing-along that would have been too much of a downer for the situation. Then they slotted a song called "Dat's What Noah Done." Earlier we mentioned that "Knock on Wood" was the only original song used in the film. Well, "Dat's What Noah Done" was supposed to be another original. The song was a rather thin, cheekily-told story of Noah's ark, written for a black entertainer singing in stereotypical racial dialogue, similar to "Shine." Though it was filmed and recorded, somewhere down the line it lost favor and got cut.

RANDOM THOUGHTS: When Strasser asks Rick whether he's in the camp of those who can't fathom their beloved Paris overrun with Germans, Rick responds that Paris is not beloved by him. Here he speaks the truth. As we will soon find out Paris holds some mighty painful memories for him.

RANDOM THOUGHTS: Rick warns Strasser not to invade certain sections of New York. We're guessing this line had New York City moviegoers cheering back in the day. To see a film rendition of New Yorkers taking it to the Nazis, find *All Through the Night* (1942). Released just a year before *Casablanca*, and featuring Bogart, Veidt and Lorre, this mad-cap affair has New York gangsters (Bogart) battling a Nazi spy ring (Veidt and Lorre). You'll have to put up with lots of dated wise-guy street slang, but it's a good-enough farce.

HISTORY LESSON: A boastful Herr Heinz asks Rick whether he can fathom London overrun with Germans. It's a curious question to ask, though, given that more than a year before this scene is set Hitler tried and failed to seize London and the rest of Great Britain.

After the Germans won the Battle of France in June 1940 with relative ease, Hitler immediately set his sights on Great Britain. The Brits knew it was coming, so much so that on June 18, 1940, Prime Minister Winston Churchill openly stated, "What General Weygand called the Battle of France is over. I expect that the Battle of Britain is about to begin. Upon this battle depends the survival of Christian civilization."

Hitler's master plan, dubbed Operation Sea Lion, called for an all-out sea-borne invasion of Britain. This was to be accomplished by first destroying the Royal Air Force, then gaining control of the English Channel, and then landing a couple hundred thousand German troops on London's doorstep.

In July 1940, the Germans commenced the battle with relentless bombing raids. At first they focused on strategic RAF targets, but quickly upped the ante by targeting London and other major cities harboring industry. Night after night, scores of Luftwaffe bombers took to the skies with the goal of bombing the British into submission. It was pure hell. But the Brits displayed awe-inspiring toughness. The turning point in the battle was on September 15, when the RAF turned back the Luftwaffe's largest raid to date. With this set back Hitler had seen enough. A few days later he effectively pulled the plug on Operation Sea Lion, and started eyeing his enemy to the east, Russia. While the Luftwaffe continued bombing runs on London and other strategic sites into May 1941, Hitler gave no more serious thought to a land invasion. All of that said, the answer to Herr Heinz's question is a resounding *no*.

DID YOU KNOW?: Explaining away Rick's somewhat evasive responses to Strasser's inquiries, Renault describes Rick as "completely neutral." Neutrality was a key principle underpinning the United States' isolationist attitudes, which of course Rick personifies. 1935 saw the United States Congress pass the first in a series of neutrality acts aimed at prohibiting the government and American citizens from aiding any country at war, making no distinction between aggressors and victims.

RANDOM THOUGHTS: Strasser's dossier on Rick turns out to be a handy reference for us as well. Rick is thirty-seven and from New York, and, for mysterious reasons, he cannot return to America. Renault thinks it's because he murdered someone and we have to admit, given Rick's slightly psychotic tendencies, a jilted-lover murder scenario is not all that far-fetched.

Here are two potential explanations for why Rick can't go home. First, Rick took up arms in not one but two foreign wars—not acceptable behavior in the eyes of the U.S. government where neutrality in foreign conflicts was the rule. Indeed, the United States invoked the Neutrality Act of 1935 against Italy and Ethiopia just months after Italy invaded Ethiopia in October 1935, while Congress passed neutrality legislation in 1937 designed to cover the Spanish Civil War. Complicating matters, Rick would have been labeled a "communist" for his choice of sides in the Spanish Civil War, and would likely have been on a U.S. government watch-list for a long time.

Second, while enjoying himself overseas during the early stages of World War II Rick could have overlooked that pesky little detail of registering for the U.S. draft. With the passage of the Selective Service and Training Act of 1940, all men who were between twenty-one and thirty-five as of October 16, 1940, were required to present themselves to the local draft board on that date. Being overseas did not get you off the hook. Sure, Rick is thirty-seven in December 1941, but it turns out he *could* have been thirty-five on October 16, 1940. All in all, Uncle Sam would have been rather upset with someone who was willing to fight for Spain but not for America.

CAST ANECDOTES: As the steely-eyed Strasser homes in on Rick it starts to sink in that this is one evil dude. Actor Conrad Veidt plays Strasser so convincingly that it's easy to believe he's every bit a German officer. Well Veidt was German all right but it's heartening to know that he was, in fact, a staunch anti-Nazi.

Veidt was a true force in German silent films during the 1920s. His most famous appearance was as a super creepy carnival sideshow somnambulist in the horror film *The Cabinet of Dr. Caligari* (1920). A cool film but, owing to youth and makeup, Veidt is unrecognizable.

In 1926, he sailed for the United States aboard the *SS Mauretania*, invited by actor John Barrymore to appear in *The Beloved Rogue* (1927). It too was a silent, made just six months before the release of the first American feature talkie, *The Jazz Singer*. He returned to his hometown of Berlin in 1929, still without a talkie to his credit.

In his absence there had been plenty of talk in Berlin, and the political and social landscape had changed dramatically. The Nazis were on the rise and publishing the foulest lies. Veidt had zero tolerance for their antics and became a vocal opponent of their hate tactics.

By early 1933, Veidt had seen enough and left for England, a decision made easier by the fact that his soon-to-be-wife was Jewish. He returned to Germany later that year for an on-location shoot, and promptly found himself a political detainee. Apparently the Nazis had not forgotten his unkind words, and were not at all amused by the fact that he had accepted the lead role in a pro-Jewish film called *The Wandering Jew*. Somehow Veidt talked his way out of that jam and wisely chose not to wander back to his homeland again.

Veidt spent the balance of the 1930s in England, during which time he managed to gain British citizenship. In June 1940, just as the Germans were marching into Rick's beloved Paris, Veidt headed back to Hollywood—this time for good.

Unfortunately, *Casablanca* was to be his penultimate film. For as healthy as Veidt looks in this scene devouring caviar and quaffing champagne, less than a year later he dropped dead on a golf course, the victim of a heart attack at the age of fifty.

MUSIC NOTES: Sam greets Victor and Ilsa with two songs upon their arrival. The first is "Speak to Me of Love," also known by the French title "Parlez-moi d'amour." The second is "Love For Sale." Two decidedly different messages sent by Sam here.

"Speak to Me of Love" is your basic "I'm-wild-about-you" love song. It was written in 1930 by a French/American duo, and popularized by the renowned French singer Lucienne Boyer. Here are words from the refrain that match the music heard:

> *Speak to me of love and say what I'm longing to hear*
> *Tender words of love repeat them again I implore you*
> *Speak to me of love and whisper these words to me*
> *Dear I adore you!*

While this song is a decent fit for Victor and Ilsa's arrival at Rick's, "Love for Sale" is another story. This Cole Porter number first appeared in the 1930 musical *The New Yorkers*. As a quick read of the lyrics will tell you, the song is about a lady of the evening shopping her wares on dim-lit corners in Manhattan. The lyrics are pretty tame, but when Billie Holiday covered the song in the 1950s many took offense. Apparently the less-than-subtle prostitution motif was too much for the powers-that-be and the song was banned from radio. Here's a sampling of the lyrics:

> *When the only sound in the empty street*
> *Is the heavy tread of the heavy feet*
> *That belong to a lonesome cop, I open shop...Love for sale*

You get the idea. Truth is, though, love is just about the only thing we *don't* see for sale in Casablanca.

EXPLANATION REQUIRED: When Ilsa asks Renault about Sam, she refers to Sam as "the boy who's playing the piano." We'd like to think she's simply referring to Sam's youthful looks, but history tells us otherwise. Yes, the script had Ilsa making one of those casual race-based references that Hollywood didn't think twice about back in the 1940s.

HISTORY LESSON: From Strasser we learn that Victor is wanted by the Third Reich for publishing an underground Resistance newspaper in Prague up until the day the Germans occupied Prague. That occurred on March 15, 1939, a dark day among many in Czech history.

But how did Prague and Czechoslovakia get on Germany's bad side in the first place? To understand this we must go back to World War I. Czechoslovakia was formed in the aftermath of the Great War, with the lofty goal of forming a democratic republic out of a handful of culturally diverse provinces. It was quite a mix—Czechs, Slovaks, Germans, Ukrainians, Hungarians—but it was not much of a melting pot. The Czechs and Slovaks pretty much hated each other, and the Germans, who made up one-fifth or so of the population, weren't exactly thrilled about their minority status.

And because the country was, geographically speaking, a sitting duck, Czechoslovakia was compelled to enter into pacts with countries historically on Germany's bad side. As Hitler rose to power in the 1930s and

Germany's master race concept continued to emerge, suddenly the notion of Germans being a minority in a country that was sidling up to France and Great Britain became intolerable.

Applying the policy of irrendentism we mentioned earlier, Hitler sought to repatriate Germans in other countries through annexation. In 1938, Hitler threatened Czechoslovakia with an all-out invasion unless it ceded to Germany the northern, and largely Germanic, Czech region of Sudetenland. In September of that year France, Italy and Great Britain, seeking to appease Hitler and avoid war in Europe, joined Germany in signing the Munich Pact. The pact handed Sudetenland over to the Germans in hopes that Hitler's land-grab aspirations would end there. But predictably, just six months later Hitler broke the pact and seized the rest of Czechoslovakia.

HISTORY LESSON: So what's the real story of the Czech Resistance during World War II? After the occupation there wasn't much resistance to speak of, even though the Czech leaders-in-exile were calling from London for an up-tick in acts of bravery. Then on May 27, 1942, two Resistance members, Jan Kubis and Josef Gabcik, stepped up and scored a monumental blow for the Czechs. These two former members of the Czech army parachuted back into their homeland on a mission to take out Reinhard Heydrich, the deputy Gestapo chief and the hand-picked "protector" of Czech-inhabited regions. They could scarcely have selected a more deserving assassination target. Heydrich had a well-earned reputation for ruthlessness—his nickname was the Hangman—and played a central role in shaping the Third Reich's so-called "Final Solution" plan to annihilate the Jewish people.

After scouting the daily route of Heydrich's car in Prague, the men waited at a hairpin turn and pulled out a semi-automatic. When the gun jammed, they went to the back-up plan and lobbed a grenade into the car. A week later Heydrich succumbed to his wounds.

Heydrich's assassination was the first in the war of a high-ranking German officer. A great feat for the Resistance to be sure, but the German reprisals were swift and devastating. The Reich placed the entire region under a state of siege, and when it was all over they had murdered some 5,000 Czech men, women and children in direct retaliation for the assassination. Two villages suspected of aiding the assassins, Lidice and Lezaky, were reduced to rubble; their residents were all shot or sent off to concentration camps. Quite understandably the reprisals had their desired effect, and for the balance of the war Czech Resistance activities were far lower in profile.

CAST ANECDOTES: *Casablanca* actor Hans Heinrich von Twardowski portrays Heydrich in *Hangman Also Die!* (1943). Von Twardowski was born in Stettin, Germany, immigrated to the United States in the early 1930s, and began appearing in Hollywood features shortly thereafter. The Allies heavily bombed Stettin at the end of World War II, destroying nearly two thirds of the city. In *Casablanca* von Twardowski plays the German officer who escorts Yvonne into the Café later in the film. We say he's far more convincing as a bad guy in *Hangman Also Die!* than he is in *Casablanca*.

DID YOU KNOW?: Once seated Victor orders the French liqueur Cointreau. A clear, orange-flavored liqueur, Cointreau is made from a mixture of peels from bitter and sweet oranges, but it's definitely more bitter than sweet. It's a nice flavoring ingredient and appears in standards such as the Cosmopolitan and the Sidecar. We can't see how Victor has it, but Cointreau is eighty proof and not particularly smooth, so we say it's better over ice.

EXPLANATION REQUIRED: Victor and Ilsa haven't even settled in before a mope-ish fellow in an ill-fitting suit approaches them. At first blush the man, who identifies himself as Berger, appears to be just another opportunistic Casablancan huckster selling jewelry to Café patrons. But after Berger flashes Victor a locket ring we instantly understand that he's been looking for Victor, and the ring is a high-sign. But are you clued in to what the ring actually signifies?

Well, the set-up for this payoff is found at the beginning of the film. Recall that the man gunned down in the market by local authorities had papers clenched in his hand that tied him to the Free France government. Recall also that those papers included the symbol of Free France—the Cross of Lorraine, a double-barred cross. That cross is precisely what appears inside the locket ring. So, a quick glance at the cross and Victor knows that he is dealing with a fellow Resistance member.

Now, anyone watching this film when it was first released would have been keen on these Free France references. But all these decades later most folks are left simply inferring that the ring tells Victor he and Berger are on the same team.

FILM ANECDOTES: As we know, *Casablanca* is full of actors whose heritage matches that of their characters. In this scene Berger reveals he's Norwegian. John Qualen played Berger, and it turns out he was a full-blooded Norwegian. Okay, so he actually was born in Canada, but no matter—his parents were both from the Land of the Midnight Sun.

Not surprisingly Qualen was tapped for more than a few Scandinavian roles during his career. His built-in sad-sack looks and demeanor had him at his best playing sympathetic, underdog characters like Berger. Qualen appears in several other film classics, including these three, all from 1940: *His Girl Friday*, a Cary Grant and Rosalind Russell screwball romantic comedy with Qualen playing the pathetic death-row inmate around whom all the quick-witted banter revolves; *The Grapes of Wrath*, with Qualen as the eccentric and wily Muley Graves, who is not going to get pushed off his God-given land without a fight; and *Knute Rockne All American*, featuring Qualen as the father of the Notre Dame football legend. Beyond these you can find Qualen in any number of John Ford westerns, including the gem *The Searchers* (1955).

EXPLANATION REQUIRED: When Renault offers Victor and Ilsa words of welcome, Victor notes that he has not been treated so cordially by the current French government, meaning the Vichy government. But left unexplained is exactly where and when Victor encountered problems with Vichy. Earlier Strasser mentions that Victor spent time in Paris carrying out his Resistance activities, so that's a possibility even though Paris was not in Vichy-controlled France.

But it's more likely that Victor had run-ins with Vichy in Marseille, when he stayed with Ilsa when she got sick (mentioned several scenes later). Marseille has always had a rough-and-tumble side to it. During the war it provided cover for refugees and Resistance members, but it also was teeming with Vichy officials. Victor could have holed up with fellow Resistance members but, out on the streets, he would have been exposed to random questioning and regular Vichy *rafles*, basically larger versions of the "usual suspects" round up we saw at the beginning of the film. Plus, at 6'3" and with a wild grey streak in his hair, Victor would have been hard to miss.

CLOSER LOOK: This evening Ilsa accessorizes her outfit with an eye-catching brooch that sparkles wildly in every shot. Interestingly, we spied this very same piece of jewelry in another Warner Bros. film. In *Hollywood Canteen* (1944), Joan Leslie wears it with equal flair and elegance.

Beyond searching for the brooch, *Hollywood Canteen* definitely is worth watching. The film is based on an actual wartime canteen that was the brainchild of actress Bette Davis, the idea being that Hollywood celebrities would mingle nightly with G.I.'s as a way of boosting morale and showing their support for the war. Not only does the film provide fascinating insight into World War II home-front goings-on, but among the parade of actors making cameo appearances in the film (as themselves) are *Casablanca* stars Sidney Greenstreet, Peter Lorre, S.Z. Sakall, Paul Henreid and Helmut Dantine.

Greensteet and Lorre scare a G.I. with some of their classic dark banter. Sakall hilariously greets each G.I. with "Good evening, General" and indulges a line of G.I.'s eager to pinch his famous jowls. Henreid washes dishes in the canteen kitchen while sharing his "ladies' man" theories on women. And Dantine? Well, he actually puts his theories on women to work by escorting the lovely Eleanor Parker to a Sunset Boulevard hot spot called Mocambo, which at the time was the place to see and be seen. Conspicuously absent from this Warner Bros. talent parade is Bogart. Though he missed out on this feel-good project, he did volunteer there from time to time.

RANDOM THOUGHTS: Upon Renault asking the waiter to bring a bottle of champagne, we learn that two employees named "Emil" work at Rick's—Emil the croupier and Emil the waiter. At least they work in different rooms.

MUSIC NOTES: As Victor and Ilsa worriedly discuss their encounter with Strasser, the house chanteuse, Señorita Andreya, takes the spotlight for a song called "Tango Delle Rose." The scene originally called for Andreya to sing two songs, with the opener being a number called "Tabu." But that song got cut to tighten things up.

Andreya sings the first part of "Tango Delle Rose" in Spanish, a plausible and logical tie-in given Morocco's connections and proximity to Spain. But, to our surprise, she sings the second part in English. The lyrics are hard to hear but, as Victor and Berger huddle at the bar, listen for the following lines: *Love is light, as the breath of the roses/If tonight, love in your heart reposes/Pluck the rose, for all of life is like a flower/Fading and dying by the hour/Fleet as a rose is love.* Sam was originally slated to introduce Señorita Andreya, but somewhere along the way the bridge got dropped.

DID YOU KNOW?: While the film's director, Michael Curtiz, does a nice job of advancing the storyline through "Tango Delle Rose," the number still feels a bit like filler. And that's for good reason, since basically it *is* filler. In 1933, President Roosevelt adopted the Good Neighbor Policy, which swore off America's interventionist tendencies and signaled cooperative times ahead. In time the policy took on particular significance with Latin American countries. With some prodding from Roosevelt, Hollywood advanced the policy by increasing the profile of Latin entertainers in film. Typically this meant writing in a part, or often a song, for a Latin type.

But also driving the scene's inclusion was the fact that World War II severely impacted Hollywood's international market. When World War II broke out in Western Europe, Hollywood suddenly lost a huge chunk of its international film audience. To compensate, studios stepped up their marketing efforts in Latin American countries.

CAST ANECDOTES: So what exotic country was Corinna Mura from? Well, America. She was born Corinna Wall in San Antonio, Texas, and grew up in Connecticut. Her mother was Scottish; her father had Spanish and English heritage. Ah, but the Latin American audiences didn't know all that.

In addition to *Casablanca*, her short-lived wartime film career had her singing numbers in *Passage to Marseille* (1944) and *Call Out the Marines* (1942). In 1944, she enjoyed a year-plus run in the Broadway musical *Mexican Hayride*, which featured Cole Porter songs and had Mura singing two numbers. A 1944 *New York Times* review noted that "Mura has a clear voice and the ability to deal with a Porter song," whatever that means. If you find yourself mesmerized by Mura's vocals, the original cast album for *Mexican Hayride*, with Mura's two songs, is still in circulation.

RANDOM THOUGHTS: At the bar, as Victor and Berger have their clandestine exchange, Victor orders a Champagne Cocktail. All you need to make this drink is a sugar cube, some Angostura bitters and, of course, champagne. Soak the cube with a few dashes of bitters, drop it into a champagne flute and pour away. The drink's flavor evolves nicely as the dissolving cube releases the bitters. And while you are sipping away, look at the bottom of Victor's glass for something swishing around that resembles a sugar cube.

EXPLANATION REQUIRED: During their exchange, Berger informs Victor that some local Resistance members will meet later that night at the *caverne du bois*. If taken literally, this means that the Cross of Lorraine gang will convene in a cave in the woods. Let's hope for comfort's sake it's just a quaint name for another Casablancan night spot.

MUSIC NOTES: Just a few notes away from reaching the film's musical centerpiece, Sam slips in another old standard. When Ilsa asks Sam to play "As Time Goes By," he's playing a wistful tune called "Avalon." The tune was among the top hits of 1920 and was also one of Benny Goodman's favorites through the years. Al Jolson co-wrote it, though he and his partner lost a lawsuit alleging they lifted the melody from the Italian opera *Tosca*.

The song is about the romantic harbor town of Avalon on California's Santa Catalina Island, a favorite weekend getaway for Hollywood celebrities back in the day. Indeed Bogart, who was an accomplished boater, regularly headed to Avalon and the coves of Santa Catalina Island on his 55-foot yacht *Santana*. Overlooking Avalon Bay is the picturesque Casino Ballroom, which was built by chewing-gum magnate William Wrigley, Jr. in 1929, when he basically owned the entire island. The ornate Art Deco ballroom became a nationally renowned hot spot for big-band dances. From the 1930s into the 1950s, couples would dance the night away—no doubt to *Avalon* and other big-band standards featured in *Casablanca*—while the rest of America listened through a national radio broadcast.

RANDOM THOUGHTS: Bogart bought *Santana* in 1945 from Hollywood couple Dick Powell and June Allyson. How attached did Bogart become to his yacht? A few years later in 1948, Bogart formed his own production company and named it Santana Productions. Later that year *Key Largo* was released, and in the film some gangsters hope to make their getaway by coercing Bogart's character into captaining a fishing boat to Cuba. The name of that boat is *Santana*. Watch *Key Largo* and it's clear that Bogart was in his element filming on and around the water. To see Bogart flashing his boating skills in other films, check out *The African Queen* (1951) and *To Have and Have Not* (1944).

MUSIC NOTES: So how did "As Time Goes By" make its way into the film? Simple. It was Rick and Ilsa's song in the original play. This scene was one of the many carry-overs from the play (though the play had Victor and Renault piano-side as well), and "As Time Goes By" came with it.

Inheriting the song may not seem like a big deal, but music directors are sensitive to having their creative options limited, and *Casablanca's* music director Max Steiner was no exception. He thought he could do better thematically but, alas, too much time had gone by. Bergman had moved on to *For Whom the Bell Tolls* and, as the story goes, already cut her hair, so the necessary reshooting of Ilsa's piano-side scene with Sam was not going to happen.

The song itself was written by Herman Hupfeld for a short-lived Broadway musical called *Everybody's Welcome*. *Time* magazine gave the "musi-comedy" a tepid review, while describing "As Time Goes By" as "tuneful" and noting that just days after the premiere, the song was all the rage in the nightclubs of Manhattan.

Keep in mind that Sam only sings the song's center cut here. Omitted are the bridge (we'll catch it later in the Paris flashback) and the song's all-but-forgotten introduction, which sets the thematic table by explaining that, however complicated the world may seem to get, we must stop from time to time to appreciate the wonderful simplicity of love. That message may have resonated with Rick in Paris, but not so much in Casablanca.

FILM ANECDOTES: One oft-cited *Casablanca* oddity is that, while the line "Play it again, Sam" is widely attributed to the film, no character actually utters those words. Interestingly, many attribute the line to Rick but it's actually Ilsa who comes closest to saying this most-famous-of-all movie misquotes. At the Café's piano Ilsa says to Sam, "Play it once Sam. For old time's sake," and then says, "Play it Sam. Play 'As Time Goes By.'"

Now, later that night Rick actually does touch on the misquote, first barking at Sam, "You played it for her, you can play it for me," and then following with, "If she can stand it I can! Play it!" But it's said in anger, which really is not the vibe that anyone attributes to the line, misquoted or not. Indeed, when the American Film Institute came out with its top 100 American film quotes (more on this later), they used Ilsa's second line, "Play it Sam. Play 'As Time Goes By.'" They could have picked the first, but either works for us.

RANDOM THOUGHTS: One lingering myth is that the "Play it again, Sam" misquote comes from the Marx Brothers' film *A Night in Casablanca* (1946). Not so. What's more, despite the teaser title, the film is not the full-on pastiche that one would expect from Groucho, Chico and Harpo.

One scene that does stand out involves the Casablanca police launching an investigation into the murder of a hotel manager. Here, the Marx Brothers cleverly cast *Casablanca* alumnus Dan Seymour—Abdul the doorman at Rick's—as the prefecture captain, effectively the equivalent of Captain Renault's role. Seymour's character then borrows from Renault's famous order, "Round up the usual suspects," changing it to, "Round up all likely suspects." Not a bad gag, particularly with Seymour doing the handy work.

In another scene, Harpo lets his money ride at a roulette table, just like the Bulgarian newlywed Jan Brandel. But the Marx Brothers inexplicably missed the obvious inside joke of having Harpo play the same number: Jan plays twenty-two, while Harpo wins on five.

CAST ANECDOTES: We love the fact that Seymour was game for this bit of Marx Brothers high jinks but between his stiff delivery and meandering, quarter-baked accent, suffice it to say you would not confuse Seymour's portrayal of Casablanca's prefect of police for Captain Renault. By the way, notwithstanding his swarthy look here, Seymour was born and raised in Chicago, which puts him on a short list of American-born actors in *Casablanca*.

Seymour appeared in another Morocco-based film in 1942, *Road to Morocco* of the Bing Crosby and Bob Hope *Road* comedy series. In that film, he has no lines and looks like Abdul's evil, bearded brother. To see Seymour in a more serious setting, check him out in two Bogart films, *Key Largo* (1948), playing a gangster henchman, and *To Have and Have Not* (1944), playing a beret-wearing local Vichy police chief.

FILM ANECDOTES: Jack Warner was none too happy to learn that the Marx Brothers were coming out with the similarly-titled *A Night in Casablanca*, and apparently had his legal wonks dash off a letter to that effect. Groucho's classic retort? The studio was using the word "Brothers" in its name without the *Marx Brothers'* permission...!

Also, several months before the Marx Brothers released their film, Jack Warner got wind that Harpo was screening *Casablanca* at his Los Angeles home without the studio's permission. He guessed that Harpo had lifted a 16mm print of the film from the War Activities Committee. Sounds like a pretty good guess.

EXPLANATION REQUIRED: A couple of things to nitpick from Rick and Ilsa's cryptic and tension-filled exchange regarding their time in Paris. First, Rick recalls that the last time they met was at a bistro called La Belle Aurore, and Ilsa adds that the Germans marched into Paris that same day. Actually, as we will discuss in a moment, the Germans reached Paris three days after the day Rick and Ilsa hung out at La Belle Aurore. Oh, well.

Moving on, Rick says he remembers that she wore blue that day and the Germans wore gray; Ilsa adds that she stopped wearing that dress because of its connection to the Germans arriving. Well, yes, the German soldiers did have gray uniforms, but as we just noted Rick didn't see them first hand. And later on we will see Ilsa in two outfits on the day Rick left Paris but neither is a dress and neither appears to be blue. In fact, she is seen wearing only one dress in Paris (while dancing) and it's not blue either. Keep an eye out for these details in the upcoming Paris flashback.

EXPLANATION REQUIRED: As Victor and Ilsa excuse themselves for the night, Renault insists on calling them a cab, adding in explanation, "Gasoline rationing. Time of night." The rationing of food, metals, gasoline, rubber and other items was standard wartime affair. In America, gasoline rationing began in seventeen states in May 1942, just days before filming started for *Casablanca*. Indeed, pre-production scripts confirm that the writers added this topical reference after filming commenced. But what exactly is Renault getting at? We gather he's saying it'll be hard to catch a cab because, one, they aren't able to roam the streets burning up fuel, and two (as Renault just mentioned) it's late and there's a curfew.

RANDOM THOUGHTS: If Victor didn't get a bad vibe from the knowing exchange between Rick and Ilsa at the table, surely he must have from Ilsa's odd comment that she saw quite a lot of Rick in Paris. What she conveniently omits is that those encounters usually took place in Rick's apartment.

CHAPTER 4

WE'LL ALWAYS HAVE PARIS

"With the whole world crumbling, we pick this time to fall in love."
—Ilsa

The last of Rick's patrons have shuffled off into the warm Casablanca night, and we find Rick inside the Café, accompanied in the darkness only by a near-empty bottle of booze and a concerned Sam. Rick is clearly thrown by Ilsa's reappearance, and when he launches into a drunken diatribe we understand that somewhere along the way Ilsa broke his heart.

In the classic self-destructive tendencies of a love-forlorn soul, Rick orders Sam to play what was once Rick and Ilsa's favorite song. The melody takes Rick back to gayer times, though the look in his eyes is one of deep despair. For us, this means drifting into "flashback mode" for a little backstory on what the heck happened between these two.

Ah, Paris. City of Light, City of Love. The perfect place for any couple—including Rick and Ilsa—to fall in love. Through his mind's eye, Rick treats us to his highlight reel of romantic times shared by the couple in Paris during the spring of 1940. A cozy drive in an open-air roadster down the Champs-Élysées and out to the bucolic French countryside, a boat ride on the River Seine, a little afternoon champagne in Rick's apartment, dancing at a local nightclub, and, finally, some late-night romancing in Ilsa's hotel room. These two sure are having fun.

But while they're in the moment, an innocent question from Rick brings to light a curious piece of information. Rick can't resist asking Ilsa how a guy like him could be lucky enough to land a dame like her. Well, confesses Ilsa, she actually was married at one time. But not to worry—he's dead now. So in Rick's mind, while she may have some emotional baggage, at least she's not taken.

Having established that Rick and Ilsa are wild about each other, what could possibly spoil these wondrous times? Well, there is that little matter of a world war going on. A short montage shows in stark terms that the Germans are on the march, and their destination is Paris. Sure enough, the next day's news is grim. The Germans will be arriving in just a few days. As Rick and Ilsa contemplate their fate at a quaint sidewalk café, we learn that Rick is a wanted man and on a German "blacklist." The situation is clear—Rick needs to leave Paris in a hurry.

Rick, Ilsa and Sam wisely decide to evacuate before the Germans arrive, but there's still time for champagne at their favorite bistro, La Belle Aurore. The German advance clearly has Ilsa spooked. Rick sees the evacuation as a perfect opportunity for the two to escape *together*, south to Marseille. But something else is weighing heavily on Ilsa's mind. Rick, oblivious to her standoffish demeanor, speaks cheerily of how soon they can get *married*—maybe as soon as *today*. Okay, forget the Germans, now Ilsa is *really* spooked.

The last train out of Paris this evening leaves at 5:00 p.m. sharp. For some reason Ilsa insists on meeting Rick at the station. Hmmm. At three minutes to five, Rick is there, but Ilsa is nowhere to be found. A minute later Sam appears. He hasn't seen Ilsa either, but explains that she did leave a note for Rick at the hotel. Well, we don't really have to read this one to know what's at hand—she's not going with Rick, now or ever. Rick is devastated and his mind races for the next move. But there is no next move. This is the *last* train out of town, and with the Germans hot on his trail he has no choice but to get on board, alone and with heavy heart.

Rick's—Main Room

RANDOM THOUGHTS: As Rick drinks and sulks he wonders what time it is in New York, and guesses that everyone in New York and America is already asleep. Unfortunately, Rick's time-zone math is a little off. Casablanca may be in Africa, but it's on the same time as London. Let's assume it's 2:00 a.m. in Casablanca. That would be mid-evening on the East Coast.

MUSIC NOTES: Sam floats out an agreeable tune and Rick demands to know what he's playing. Sam replies that it's just something he made up. Actually, that's not far from reality. Though this song has an odd familiarity to it, it's just a snippet from an instrumental—it doesn't even have a name—that Warner Bros. obtained from a musician for the thrifty price of one dollar.

FILM ANECDOTES: Of the film's countless collectibles, the most coveted is almost certainly the upright piano from the Café. It was owned for years by a private collector who, as he tells it, on a hunch scooped it up from a prop house for next to nothing, and then stripped off various layers of paint to reveal the piano's unmistakable original salmon color and Moroccan-inspired design details. Its value was anyone's guess until 2014 when it finally went under the hammer for a whopping $3.4 million.

But if you think about it, Sam plays two pianos—one in Casablanca at the Café, and another in Paris at La Belle Aurore. So what happened to the one from the Paris flashback? Well, in the early 1980s, the same collector who owned the Café piano acquired the La Belle Aurore piano, also from a prop house. In 1988, he sold the green and beige, 58-key piano at auction for $154,000 to an undisclosed Japanese buyer. In 2012, the buyer put it back on the auction block and this time it sold for $602,000.

So why is the La Belle Aurore piano a bargain compared to the Café piano? Well, for one the Café piano gets a lot more screen time, circulating the room like it's one of the main characters. It also literally sets the mood in several key Café scenes. And according to the auction house behind the 2014 sale, the Café piano's desirability gets a huge boost from its close scene ties to the film's central construct—obtaining the letters of transit to escape Casablanca—with Rick even using the piano as the hiding place for the letters themselves. That said, the La Belle Aurore piano has its own special place in the film and we're betting that next time around someone is going to pay up big time for its connection to Rick and Ilsa's idyllic Paris romance.

Paris—Day Scenes

CLOSER LOOK: We know instantly that Rick's alcohol-assisted flashback is based in Paris by two shots of the Arc de Triomphe. It sits at the west end of Paris' most famous thoroughfare, the Champs-Élysées, smack in the middle of a twelve-road rotary. The arch is Napoleon's tribute to his army, and features four high-relief sculptures depicting various war-themed events.

In the first shot of the arch, we can make out just enough detail of the two relief sculptures to confirm that we're looking at the Champs-Élysées side of the monument. In the second shot, the same two sculptures confirm that Rick and Ilsa are driving down the Champs-Élysées, headed toward Place de la Concorde and Musée du Louvre.

The cars in both shots give the film clips away as pre-1940s vintage, with the first one being from perhaps as early as the late 1920s. So we will call this a gaffe for failing to plausibly match stock footage to the film's setting.

RANDOM THOUGHTS: Taking things a step further, we were hoping to pin down the building and precise window from which the establishing footage of the arch was taken. The aforementioned relief sculptures on the arch confirm that the shot was from a building on the south side of the Champs-Élysées, just a few blocks down from the arch. Alas, a review of the building history for the stretch, together with a site visit, leads us to conclude that the perch used is no longer there.

HISTORY LESSON: It's hard to believe, but just days after Rick and Ilsa made this drive, a Nazi flag was flying from the arch, German troops were high-stepping down the Champs-Élysées and Hitler was cruising the very same route. On June 23, 1940, the day after France signed the armistice with Germany, Hitler flew into town for an unannounced early-morning three-hour whirlwind tour of Paris. Included in the tour was a ride on the Champs-Élysées and a spin around the arch. Despite his obsession with Paris, he never visited again.

RANDOM THOUGHTS: That's a sporty English roadster Rick is driving. But seeing as the French drive on the right side of the road, it would help to have the steering wheel on the left. **(39:01)**

FILM ANECDOTES: At one point the writers had Ilsa delivering this eye-rolling line during the roadster clip: "When I am driving with you, I don't know if I am in the city or on a country lane." Director Curtiz had the good sense to drop the line, but when producer Wallis got word he complained about not being consulted. If Wallis fancied the line, it would have been the rare bad call for him during production. But even if Wallis had prevailed, it probably wouldn't have mattered. Bergman saved a few other dud lines during the film, and surely would have saved this one.

A modern-day view of the section of Pont Rouelle that appears in the Paris flashback.

CLOSER LOOK: Rick and Ilsa's boat cruise on the Seine got us thinking it would be neat to pinpoint the spot on the river where this superimposed scene occurs.

Well, thanks to some distinguishing features on the bridge in the background, as well as a big assist from the Eiffel Tower, we can confirm that our Parisian lovers are on a boat that's just south of a bridge named Pont Rouelle. This is a train bridge located between Seine bridges Pont de Grenelle and Pont de Bir-Hakeim—you can just make out Pont de Bir-Hakeim farther on in the distance.

Armed with this information, you can recreate this shot with your significant other by throwing on some tailored suits similar to the ones worn by Rick and Ilsa, jumping on a Seine boat tour, and waiting for just the right moment to snap that photo. Or if you'd rather stay on terra firma, you can roughly simulate the view in the film from below Pont de Grenelle; just head down the stairs to the island, Île aux Cygnes. And while you're down there, make sure you track down the quarter-scale replica of—surprise, surprise—the Statue of Liberty.

Paris—Rick's Apartment

DID YOU KNOW?: All the romantic Parisian activities have Rick and Ilsa feeling quite amorous, so they head over to Rick's apartment (this is known only from the script) for some bubbly. We know Rick is a suave guy, but how are his skills opening a bottle of champagne? For champagne purists, the basic goal would be to prevent any mousse from escaping, more to save content than any effect on taste. The best way to do this is to hold the cork firmly with one hand while slowly turning the bottle with the other. Then, to disperse the pressure release, tilt the cork as it starts to exit. Ah, but sometimes the moment calls for a festive pop of the cork. Here, Rick achieves the best of both worlds. He launches the cork, but with no mousse lost and the desired effect on his audience—Ilsa is all giggles.

Paris—Nightclub

MUSIC NOTES: Rick and Ilsa put the war behind them for the evening at a Parisian nightclub, ballroom dancing to "Perfidia," a swingy song with exotic roots. Written by Mexican composer Alberto Dominguez in 1939, the Latin-based tune soon became a big band staple, with big band leaders Xavier Cugat, Glenn Miller, Benny Goodman and Jimmy Dorsey all covering the song in the brink-of-war era. Of these, Cugat had the most success with it, hitting No. 3 in March 1941. "Perfidia" was in vogue by June 1940 when this scene is set, so no timing gaffe here.

Curious thing about "Perfidia," though. Despite its romantic vibe, the lyrics are a definite downer. It's about a guy who's just discovered the love of his life in the arms of another man. Well, *perfidious* does mean *treacherous* and *faithless*, so this certainly makes sense. Anyway, his heart broken, he ends with: *And now I know my love was not for you/And so I'll take it back with a sigh/Perfidious one, good-bye.* Hmmm. A bit of foreshadowing, it seems, for Rick and Ilsa. Post-Paris, the song pretty well sums up Rick's feelings for Ilsa.

CLOSER LOOK: In this scene and throughout the film, Rick wears a ring on the fourth finger of his right hand. This is a gem-studded ring that Bogart inherited from his father, and it's visible in a slew of his films. Oddly, though, in this scene we spied a ring on the fourth finger of Rick's left hand. **(40:08)**

Paris—Ilsa's Hotel Room

RANDOM THOUGHTS: Rick and Ilsa wear different outfits in each montage vignette, which points to the montage covering more than one day. Both dress quite spiffily throughout, with Rick always in a suit or jacket. He sets out on their drive in a light-colored tweed jacket, sports a light-colored pinstripe suit for the boat ride, dons a dark pinstripe suit in his apartment, flashes a tuxedo at the nightclub and, finally, reprises the dark pinstripe in Ilsa's hotel room.

Ilsa's outfits are all fetching, naturally, with our favorite being the one she wears dancing—an alluring, puff-sleeved sheer dress, adorned with what, on close inspection, prove to be playful heart-shaped leaves. A fine choice for the romantic moment.

JUST WONDERING: We appreciate the couple's desire to set a romantic mood, but a roaring fire in Paris in June? Could be a little toasty.

World War II Montage

CLOSER LOOK: The montage of the German army sweeping into Paris contains some interesting stock wartime footage. In one shot, German troops cross a river on a makeshift bridge. A closer look reveals that there are more horses than troops, and most of the troops are making use of bicycles. Horses make sense, but what's with the bicycles? Well, in wartime any means for transporting troops is in play, even for the creators of the blitzkrieg, and the Germans made full use of bicycle infantries. Still, it's hard not to smile at the thought of a soldier having to break out the old bike pump mid-advance, tripped up by the inevitable flat tire.

DID YOU KNOW?: Next up in the montage is a highlight reel of German military fire power. Let's do a quick run through the stock footage of German tanks and planes. First seen is a seemingly endless line of tanks rolling through the French countryside. These particular tanks are Panzers, as in *Panzerkampfwagen*, as in "armored fighting vehicle." And this particular tank division—the Germans had six, with each containing a couple hundred tanks—is stocked with Panzer IIs. Despite being a second-generation tank the Panzer IIs were still a little light in weight and armament. But in the Battle of France a superior battle plan allowed the tanks to outmaneuver more technically advanced French tanks.

Pause the film to see a vehicle commander perched in the tank's turret, leering at the camera through his shaded bug-eyed goggles. **(41:32)** More than six decades later this very same clip resurfaced in the superb World War II documentary *Rape of Europa* (2006), used similarly in a montage portraying the German invasion of France.

The first of four clips of German planes features a low-flying Junker Ju-87 "Stuka" dive-bomber, still carrying two bombs beneath its wings. **(41:36)** Stukas were the terror of the skies throughout the war, although during the Battle of Britain the RAF exposed them as lacking in the pure dogfight category. It was terrifying enough for Allied forces to see waves of bomb-carrying Stukas hurtling down at them in near-vertical dives. But the Germans also engaged in psychological warfare by equipping the planes with a wind-driven siren that produced a sound—dubbed the Trumpets of Jericho—that would have you convinced the world was ending.

The second plane is a Messerschmitt Bf-110, a bomber and night-fighter featured by the Germans in the Battle of France. Check out the gaping shark mouth painted on the plane's nose—a signature motif of the Mediterranean-based Luftwaffe fighter group known as the Haifischgruppe. **(41:37)**

Next up is a swarm of the aforementioned Stukas, no doubt scouring the fields for an Allied tank brigade suitable for strafing. **(41:38)** Finally, the last plane is a Heinkel He 111, the Luftwaffe's go-to bomber throughout the war and the main culprit terrorizing London during the Battle of Britain. This plane had a crew of five, and you can see four of them in this shot. The pilot, navigator/bombardier and nose gunner are all up front, while the dorsal gunner is on top, facing backwards. **(41:39)**

Paris—Sidewalk Café

CLOSER LOOK: Newspapermen scurry about selling copies of a special edition of Paris' leading newspaper, *Paris-Soir*, shouting variously in French, "Ask for Paris-Soir!" "Order to evacuate!" "Special edition, Paris-Soir! "Order of evacuation!" "Paris-Soir, Mister! Order of Evacuation, Mister." One newspaperman hands Rick a newspaper and, despite the confusion, Rick does in fact pay for it. **(41:50)**

EXPLANATION REQUIRED: Time for another French lesson, this time translating the front page of *Paris-Soir*. The main headline translates to *Paris Open City*. This refers to the fact that the French command, having seen the Germans level Warsaw when the Polish army tried to defend it in September 1939, decided that the only way to save Paris was to leave it undefended.

On the left, another headline translates to *Cowardly Aggression–Italy Declares War on Us*. This headline mocks Italian leader Benito Mussolini for his decision to declare war on France only after Germany's victory over France was all but in the bag. Mussolini, it seems, had not anticipated a German rout, and was left scrambling to position Italy for a piece of the spoils of war.

Lower down, a headline translates to *A Blow with a Dagger to the Back, Declares President Roosevelt*. This headline refers to some pointed words Roosevelt had for Mussolini regarding his aforementioned cowardly act of aggression.

HISTORY LESSON: Now that we're up to speed on this day's grim war news, let's see if these three headlines match up with how things were actually unfolding in Paris in June 1940. The date on the newspaper's masthead reads Tuesday, June 11, 1940. At that moment one faction of the German army had captured Reims ninety miles northeast of Paris, while another one was less than eighty miles northwest of Paris, having captured Rouen a few days earlier. Still, the French government did not declare Paris an open city (as the headline proclaims) until June 13. So time-wise the *Paris Open City* headline is premature by at least two days.

Next, the *Italy Declares War* headline does check out—Italy actually did declare war on France the previous day, June 10. Finally, the *Dagger to the Back* headline also checks out. The quote spawns from what has become known, appropriately enough, as Roosevelt's "Dagger to the Back Speech." He delivered that speech at a University of Virginia commencement ceremony on June 10, just hours after Italy declared war on France.

Before then Italy had been content watching the war in Western Europe from the sidelines. While Roosevelt tried every diplomatic trick in the book to broker a neutrality deal between Italy, Great Britain and France, Mussolini's ties to Hitler proved too deep. Now, with a German victory over France assured, Mussolini decided the time was right to jump on the bandwagon.

In the speech Roosevelt thoroughly undressed Mussolini for his transgressions before declaring, with a weight and intensity that only Roosevelt could summon: "On this tenth day of June, 1940, the hand that held the dagger has struck it into the back of its neighbor." The speech marked a clear break from America's position of neutrality, with Roosevelt delivering harsh words for the "delusional" thinking of isolationist-minded Americans, and promising to any and all "opponents of force" (meaning any country that had incurred the wrath of Germany and Italy) the "material resources" of the United States.

FILM ANECDOTES: Film lore has it that the newspaper used in this scene is an actual copy of *Paris-Soir* from June 11, 1940, contributed by the film's technical advisor, Robert Aisner. A great anecdote, if true, especially considering that the June 11 edition of *Paris-Soir* was the last one published in Paris before the publisher abruptly closed shop and headed south to safety. But, remember, we already confirmed that one of the headlines is two days premature, plus there are multiple copies floating around this scene.

Knowing this, there was no real need to track down the actual June 11, 1940, edition of *Paris-Soir*. But we did anyway. While a couple of editions were printed that day (no surprise), none of them match up with what we now know is a prop. We can say, though, that the prop department definitely had a recent copy of *Paris-Soir* in hand when it made this thing. The layout and fonts match up remarkably well with that of actual editions of *Paris-Soir*. So perhaps Aisner did contribute a recent copy.

CLOSER LOOK: While we were examining the paper handed to Rick we discovered, to our amazement, that the headlines on the back page are actually in English. That's right, among the barely-legible headlines are these two U.S.-themed headlines: *Match Play Opens in P.G.A. Links Tourney* and *Federal Reserve Reports Changes*. Another informs that a new governmental cabinet is set to declare a policy. See if your eyes are keen enough to decipher any others.

Now, the newspaperman who hands the paper to Rick is definitely selling *Paris-soir* newspapers—the front page of the paper he sells to the customer just before Rick is visible long enough to confirm that it bears the same *Paris-soir* headline visible on other copies floating around this scene. So what's going on here—U.S. headlines in a Paris newspaper?

Well, it appears the film's prop team modified a studio-created U.S. newspaper mock up, with just the front page changed here to the *Paris-soir* format. It's possible that Bogart was supposed to keep the paper folded in half in order to hide the U.S. headlines on the back page. Regardless, someone watching the dailies for this scene should have noticed that the back-page headlines were legible on film.

We spied this *PGA* headline in newspaper props used in a few other films, including *Crossfire* (1947). Interestingly, the headline actually matches up with real-world events going on at the time Warner Bros. filmed these scenes. The 1942 PGA Championship's tournament format called for two days of stroke play, with the top thirty-two players qualifying for the single-elimination, match play portion of the tournament. Match play opened on May 27, and the filming dates for the Paris flashback scenes included May 27. Golf legend Sam Snead won that war-era tournament, and, true to the times, just a few days later he started serving in the Navy.

CLOSER LOOK: Okay, back to the front page for a few more snippets. The upper left corner of the masthead reads *La Guerre–Souscrivez*, or *The War–Subscribe*; subscribe, that is, to war bonds. But with France just days away from a de facto surrender, it's a little late for a war-bond drive.

The center column beneath the main headline reads *Avis a la Population*, which basically means *public notice*. While the notice's content undoubtedly is somber, it ends with an upbeat and patriotic *"Vive La France! Vive La Nation!"* The column on the left reads *Ordre D'Evacuation*. This, of course, translates to *Get the Heck Out of Town*. Indeed, Parisians had been leaving town in increasing numbers in early June on news of the Germans creeping ever closer. Reality set in for the holdout citizenry on this 11th day of June when the French government pulled up stakes and made a dash for the city of Tours, more than a hundred miles to the southwest. With that clear signal, Paris went into full-blown evacuation mode. Shops, apartments, personal possessions were abandoned. The main streets heading south out of Paris jammed with a sea of loaded-down pedestrians, vehicles, carts, animals, bicycles and the like. By June 13, the streets of Paris were empty. One more night, and the Germans would arrive to break the silence.

CLOSER LOOK: Just after the shot of the newspaper, look all the way down the street for a poster that reads *Chocolat Menier*. **(41:45)** This French chocolatier was founded in 1816, and since 1825 had been cranking out chocolate confectionaries in a suburb just east of Paris called Noisiel. Chocolat Menier was flying high in the 1800s and early 1900s, but the economic turmoil of both world wars took its toll on the company. Through a series of acquisitions, the original Noisiel factory eventually fell into the hands of French confectionery giant Nestle, and the architecturally impressive facility now serves as Nestle's headquarters.

Chocolat Menier is perhaps best known for its iconic poster advertisement of a little girl on her tiptoes scrawling the company name on a wall with a stick of chocolate. That poster came about in 1893 when, in a stroke of advertising genius, the company commissioned French artist Firmin Bouisset to design a child-based poster advertisement. The result was not only an advertising smash, but also a masterpiece in French poster art. Indeed, the poster became part of a famed turn-of-the-century series of French poster art known as *Les Maîtres de l'Affiche*. Unfortunately, for some reason the prop team chose not to use the famous poster, depicting instead the company name only, sans illustrations.

CLOSER LOOK: In the foreground stands a Morris column plastered with advertisements and public notices. **(41:45)** Named after the company that builds them, the columns have been a ubiquitous and iconic feature on the walkways of Paris since 1868. This particular column is adorned with cigarette ads. Although the ads are partially covered by other postings, one is definitely for Gitane, a popular low-end French cigarette brand. If the entire poster was visible you would almost surely see a dancing gypsy—*gitane* is French for gypsy, and caricatures of gypsies were mainstays in Gitane ads. Posted over the cigarette ads are official government notices, titled *République Française*, no doubt alerting Parisians to the fact that their city is now open, and instructing them to leave town immediately.

EXPLANATION REQUIRED: Rick and Ilsa's café is called Café Pierre. There is no specific reference in the film to Café Pierre's location in Paris, but the film script reveals that it's at the top of Montmartre, the storied hill district known for its artistic bohemian bent.

Warner Bros. actually did a nice job capturing the look and feel of Montmartre. Head to the top of Montmartre and you can find sidewalk cafés and bistros with wood-beamed ceilings closely resembling the ones in these scenes. But if you want to see where they actually filmed the exterior Montmartre scenes, you'll have to go to Burbank, California, and find the back-lot street at Warner Bros. still known as, appropriately enough, French Street.

CLOSER LOOK: Signage in Café Pierre's window reads *Aperitifs—Liqueurs de Marque*. In a later scene you can just see a sign above the café also touting wine (*vins*). Also visible on the café's façade is a poster advertisement for Folies Bergère, an actual Parisian cabaret located not far from Montmartre. This institution has been around since 1869, and has hosted some rather sensual acts through the years, including Josephine Baker's famed banana dance of the 1920s. If Rick and Ilsa are looking for some nighttime entertainment and don't mind some artful exposure, it's either here or the equally famous Moulin Rouge.

EXPLANATION REQUIRED: Here's the unsettling message conveyed by the Germans to Parisians via a loudspeaker van:

> Here, from Stuttgart, Germany. French-Parisians!
> The French troops have abandoned their positions.
> The Germans will be at the capital tomorrow.

Rick somehow knows French—he correctly remarks that the Germans will be in Paris by Wednesday (which is tomorrow), though his "Thursday at the latest" remark is not part of the announcement.

JUST WONDERING: We're never told how Rick came to be on the Germans' "blacklist," but we have a pretty good idea. Rick's involvement in the Spanish Civil War would pretty well have done the trick. Remember, the Loyalists (Rick's side) lost to the fascist and Hitler-backed Nationalists. After the German occupation of France in 1940, those Loyalists who had taken up residence in France found themselves on the Gestapo's blacklist, political enemies of the Third Reich. So Rick definitely was in danger of being "chucked" into a French prison.

Paris—La Belle Aurore

CLOSER LOOK: La Belle Aurore, which means The Beautiful Dawn, is a cozy little upstairs bistro, complete with exposed wooden beams, checkered tablecloths, straight-backed chairs and Sam playing a stand-up piano. A bistro called The Beautiful Dawn seems like an appropriate setting given Rick and Ilsa's budding relationship, but might the sun soon be setting on this torrid affair?

JUST WONDERING: Is it just us, or are Rick and Ilsa a little too casual about the whole German invasion thing? As we are about to learn, German artillery is within earshot, but there's still time for a champagne party? We say, drop the glasses now and head for the train station while there's still time.

EXPLANATION REQUIRED: The urgency of the situation points to this La Belle Aurore scene taking place on the same day as the preceding Café Pierre scene. With the loudspeaker's alert that the Germans will arrive tomorrow, there's no way Rick and Ilsa would stick around town until tomorrow evening, hoping that the Germans arrive behind schedule. It's slightly curious that they wear different outfits in the scenes (Rick's suit may be the same but his tie and lapel flower change), but that just means they changed for their afternoon meet-up with Sam and pending travel.

CLOSER LOOK: Resting on the bar is a glass holder in the shape of the Eiffel Tower. Complete with three levels for storing glassware, this intriguing piece is sure to be claimed as a war trophy by a soon-to-arrive German soldier.

CLOSER LOOK: The bistro's walls are adorned with various drawings, paintings and posters. Two famous French art posters are clearly visible in the scene. The first one appears when Rick walks from the bar back to the piano. On the back wall hangs a poster that reads Eugénie Buffet. **(42:41)** Eugénie Buffet was a wildly popular turn-of-the-century Parisian chanteuse, and this poster advertises her performances at Les Ambassadeurs, a cabaret located on the Champs-Élysées. Close scrutiny reveals the amusing fact that this is not a print of the original but, rather, a close remake.

The second one, which appears behind Rick just after Ilsa promises to meet him at the station, is a remake of the famous *Divan Japonais* art poster by Henri de Toulouse-Lautrec. **(45:22)** This poster's appearance is appropriate not only because Toulouse-Lautrec was practically the mayor of Montmartre, but also because the poster's setting, a cabaret called Divan Japonais, was located in the heart of Montmartre. Incidentally, both posters are part of the famed *Les Maîtres de l'Affiche* poster art series, the same one that includes the *Chocolat Menier* poster we mentioned earlier.

CLOSER LOOK: Another local newspaper, *Le Petit Parisien,* appears in the foreground of this scene. The headline on the left translates to *We Will Not Defend Paris.* The one on the right translates to *The Fatherland In Danger.* As with *Paris-Soir, Le Petit Parisien* was an actual newspaper circulating in Paris in June 1940. And just like the *Paris-Soir* paper shown a few scenes earlier, this one is a mock-up. Again, the masthead and page layout are the "tells." For the sake of completeness, the headline for the actual June 11, 1940 edition of *Le Petit Parisien* did address Italy's June 10 war declaration, reading, in French of course, *Italy Declares War On Allies.*

MUSIC NOTES: Here Sam gives us a nice reprise of "As Time Goes By," except that we are in flashback mode, so technically it's not a reprise. This time around Sam plays the song's bridge, which we have not yet heard. We're sure Sam knows this one by heart so the music sheet perched on the piano must be for some other song.

CLOSER LOOK: Take a moment to peruse the illustration we constructed of the Montmartre block featured in this scene. Located on one end of the block is Rick and Ilsa's Café Pierre. Next door is a bookstore (*librairie*) owned by one E. Pachot. One down from there is a watch and jewelry store, owned by one Dupuy, with signage that translates to, House of Gold, Silver and Platinum. Next to that store is a hat shop (signage, *Modes-Chapellerie*, not in film).

The store at the end of the block has an advertisement on its façade urging Parisians to go to Louis' (*Allez Chez Louis*). A common French restaurant naming convention is *Chez* followed by the owner's name, so it's a good bet the advertisement is referring to Louis' restaurant. Still, it's unclear whether the corner store is supposed to be Louis'. The signage above the store's door includes *midi* (midday or south) but otherwise is not fully legible in the film. Whatever, we think the corner store is a restaurant.

Interestingly, the *Allez Chez Louis* advertisement is missing moments earlier when Rick and Ilsa sit at Café Pierre. In its place hangs the *Chocolat Menier* poster.

True to Montmartre's hilly terrain, the stores are fronted by a stepped walkway that slopes upward toward Café Pierre.

Finally, we can place La Belle Aurore in the same area, and determine how it orients to the stores, based on Rick and Ilsa's view of the loudspeaker van out the bistro's window.

CLOSER LOOK: While Veuve Clicquot is the only champagne mentioned by name in the film, all the screen time goes to champagne from the house of G.H. Mumm. Here, Sam, Rick and Ilsa enjoy the first of four bottles of Mumm Cordon Rouge they have slated for consumption. **(43:02)** Cordon Rouge bottles are easily identified by their distinctive red ribbon, representing the red sash of the French Legion of Honor. You can also spy bottles of Cordon Rouge in Rick's apartment during the Paris flashback, and in Rick's Café, including when the German officers briefly take control of the house entertainment on the second night. **(1:12:57)**

DID YOU KNOW?: In 2005, the American Film Institute came out with its top 100 movie quotes of all time. A whopping six were from *Casablanca*. *The Wizard of Oz* and *Gone With the Wind* had the next most with a mere three apiece. Of the six, "Here's looking at you, kid" earned the highest rank at No. 5. Here are the others that made the list:

"Louis, I think this is the beginning of a beautiful friendship." (No. 20)

"Play it Sam. Play 'As Time Goes By.'" (No. 28)

"Round up the usual suspects." (No. 32)

"We'll always have Paris." (No. 43)

"Of all the gin joints in all the towns in all the world, she walks into mine." (No. 67)

EXPLANATION REQUIRED: You don't have to know German to figure out that the second loudspeaker announcement of the day is plain old bad news. Still, here's the message our German invaders have for their soon-to-be subjects:

Frenchmen. Frenchmen. Citizens of Paris. Listen very closely!
The German troops are standing at the gates of Paris.
Your resistance is useless. Your army is about to be dissolved.
Don't be concerned, we will restore peace and order.

The announcement then trails off, with Rick and Ilsa speaking over it. If you can figure that part out, by all means let us know.

CLOSER LOOK: This news is announced via a French government loudspeaker van. The side of the van reads French Republic (*République Française*). The passenger side door reads P.T.T. 12—Service Radio. PTT stands for Post, Telegraph and Telephone, the French public agency then in charge of such services. It's not surprising that the PTT would be in charge of alerting the citizens of Paris to the German advance, but it does seem a little odd that the PTT is already carrying official German announcements.

JUST WONDERING: Come to think of it, what good is an announcement to Parisians about how to act when the announcement is not in French? Let's hope that, like Ilsa, these folks are up on their German.

RANDOM THOUGHTS: So how old is the fresh-faced Ilsa in the film? No way of knowing exactly, but some dialogue in this scene gives us a decent idea, and she's a youngster. When Rick asks Ilsa where she was ten years ago, Ilsa replies that she was getting braces. If we assume that Ilsa's orthodontic work occurred when she was around, say, twelve, that would make her twenty-two in the Paris flashback. Then tack on another year and a half for the post-Paris era, and that puts her at around twenty-three or four.

PARIS FLASHBACK—MONTMARTRE STREET

1. Rick and Ilsa's outdoor table at Café Pierre.
2. Wall where *Chocolate Menier* poster and *Allez Chez Louis* signage visible.
3. Where loudspeaker van is parked for both announcements regarding the advancing Germans.
4. Rick grabs a bottle of champagne at the bar in La Belle Aurore.
5. Sam, Rick and Ilsa at the piano, with Sam playing "As Time Goes By."
6. Rick and Ilsa look out a window, down toward the loudspeaker van.
7. Rick and Ilsa discuss their future and plans to leave Paris.

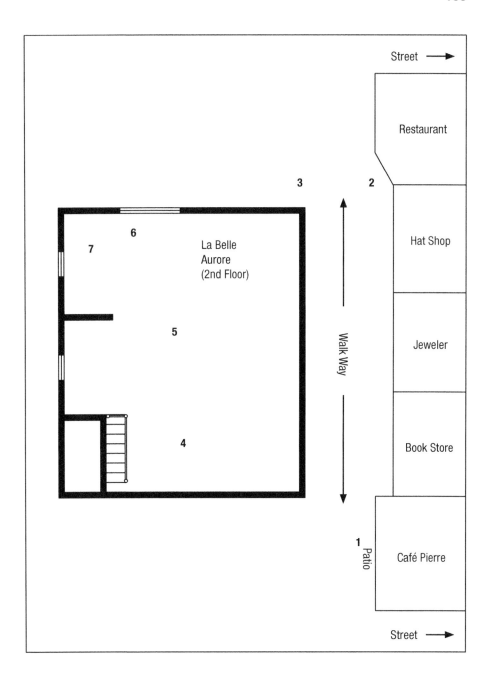

DID YOU KNOW?: As the artillery shells explode just miles from Paris, Rick comments knowingly that they are hearing the "new German 77." This is a reference to a piece of field artillery used by the Germans during World War I—the 77 refers to the diameter, in millimeters, of the shells that it fired. The Germans did use the 77 in World War II, but eventually replaced it with more powerful guns.

So why does Rick say "the *new* German 77"? Well, film lore has it that this was a bit of Warner Bros. film propaganda designed to trick the Germans into thinking that the Allies weren't wise to the German 88-millimeter field gun. We're not buying it. The existence of the 88 was hardly a secret—the Germans introduced the first generation in the mid-1930s, and the gun saw use during in the Spanish Civil War. Whatever, there is no doubt that the 88 was the star artillery piece for the Germans during World War II.

RANDOM THOUGHTS: On June 12, the day after Rick and Ilsa hear the approaching German artillery, *The United Press* ran a short piece affirming Rick and Ilsa's experience: "Residents in the outer parts of [Paris] reported hearing the roar of the night-battle and seeing the gun flashes on the northwestern horizon."

CLOSER LOOK: Ilsa wears a smart herringbone suit, ideal for traveling. The outfit comes with a barely-visible accessory, a pill-box hat resting on the table. **(44:36)** And we say we'd rather see it there than on Ilsa's head. The beret Ilsa wears in Café Pierre is the essence of bohemian Montmartre. But a pill-box? Not so much.

DID YOU KNOW?: Despite Ilsa displaying all the eye contact of a coyote, Rick has such a good feeling about their future that he floats the idea of getting married by the train engineer on the way to Marseille. Rick theorizes that if a ship's captain can do that sort of thing, why not a train engineer?

So does a ship's captain really have any special authority to marry a couple? Nope. A ship's captain certainly can preside over a marriage ceremony, it's just that for the ceremony to have any binding effect the captain would have to have separate credentials to solemnize marriages. Short of that, the ceremony could hold up because the couple met the requirements of a common law marriage. As for Rick and Ilsa, it really doesn't matter who they use—given Ilsa's soon-to-be revealed secret, it won't count. Ah, but again, we are getting ahead of ourselves.

RANDOM THOUGHTS: Here's a tip. If you ever float to your girl the idea of eloping, and she responds with mutterings along the lines of how crazy the world is and how anything can happen, and then says "Kiss me as if it were the last time," the odds are pretty good it *will* be the last time. At least for now, Ilsa looks pretty well convinced that this is the end of the line for her and Rick.

CAST ANECDOTES: Despite Bogart landing a kiss so loaded with passion that it sends a champagne glass flying **(46:32)**, Bergman always insisted that she had no romantic chemistry with Bogart. In her words, she kissed him but never knew him. Who knows why the two lacked chemistry, but surely it didn't help that in this scene and others Bogart offers up quite a wet lip.

Paris—Train Station

EXPLANATION REQUIRED: Looks like Rick is not the only one in Paris to hit on the notion of leaving town. The scene at the train station is pure chaos. A station attendant urges travelers to hustle up, else they'll miss the last train. Here's what he says, in French: "Get in the train car! Get in the train car! There are only three minutes! Let's go, get in the train car! There are only three minutes here! Let's press! Get in the train car. It is the last train!"

A woman pleads with the attendant, "And my little boy, and my little boy." Whatever the issue is, the attendant has no time to help her. Finally, watch the attendant receive an unexpected shove from an increasingly anxious Rick. **(46:44)**

CLOSER LOOK: Several station signs help set the scene. One overhead and in the background identifies the station as Gare de Lyon, which is in fact the Paris station you depart from if, like Rick, you're headed for southeastern France and Marseille.

Another sign, overhead in the foreground, translates to Pathway—Forbidden to Cross the Tracks (*Passage–Interdit de Traverser les Voies*). A sign on the right informs travelers that the import taxation and packages booths are all the way down on the right (*Octroi et Colis au Fond à Droite*). Another instructs that baggage claim is at the third counter on the left (*Enregistrement des Bagages 3eme Guichet à Gauche*).

On the train there's more signage. One car is designated for refugees (*Réfugiés*) and is also marked as a sleeping car (*Voiture-Lits*). In June 1940, the term *refugee* would apply to millions of displaced inhabitants of Belgium, the Netherlands, Luxembourg, Germany and elsewhere fleeing to southern France in advance of the German army. In the windows are signs reading Direction Marseille, Red Cards (*Cartes Rouges*) and Green Cards (*Cartes Vertes*).

DID YOU KNOW?: Above the train's windows is the name of the railway, Société Nationale des Chemins de Fers Français or SNCF. SNCF was France's national railway back in 1940, and it still exists today. As the train pulls out you can see the company's logo—the letters SNCF—flash by. **(47:51)**

Several decades after World War II, SNCF found itself under fire for its role in a Nazi deportation scheme that resulted in more than 76,000 people, nearly all Jews, being deported from France to German concentration camps. SNCF trains were used to transport the victims, with less than 3,000 surviving. Lawsuits accused the railway of being complicit in crimes against humanity and sought reparations. SNCF insisted its involvement was attributable to orders from the Vichy government and Nazi threats of death reprisals. In 2010, SNCF issued a statement expressing sorrow and regret for its role in the deportations. More recently, a U.S. lawsuit filed against SNCF resulted in France paying $60 million into a reparations settlement fund for deportation survivors and their spouses and descendants.

CLOSER LOOK: In the first shot of the station an older man carrying a child and her doll shuffles past Rick and the station clock. **(46:37)** But after passing out of view screen left, notice that the man circles around and walks in front of Rick a second time. **(46:53)** Hmmm. We know the goal here is to create a chaotic atmosphere, but this looks to us like the work of an over-eager extra.

FILM ANECDOTES: The film's production materials indicate that Warner Bros. saved a few bucks on this scene by reusing a train station set built for *Now, Voyager*, a film still in production when filming began on *Casablanca*. Well, curiosity got the best of us and we wanted to see whether the sets were at all similar. A screening of this romantic melodrama, which stars Bette Davis and *Casablanca* stars Claude Rains and Paul Henreid, confirmed that the sets are the same. The main giveaways are the fencing and the steel beams. So just swap out the station sign used in *Now, Voyager* for one that reads Gare de Lyon, add a few other French signs, and you've got a Paris train station suitable for Rick's unhappy sendoff.

RANDOM THOUGHTS: A few more tidbits on *Now, Voyager* relating to *Casablanca*. First, the similarity between Henreid's train departure in *Now, Voyager* and Bogart's in *Casablanca* is unmistakable. Filmed just months apart and, as we now know, on the same set, both scenes have the men striking mournful poses in the gangway of a coach car as dramatic Max Steiner-scored music ushers their heavy hearts down the tracks.

Second, both films use the song "Perfidia" in the same way, with the star couples dancing cheek-to-cheek on the dance floor. Finally, we were quite amused to see Henreid's character in *Now, Voyager* ordering Cointreau for him and his lady, just as Victor does in Rick's Café.

CLOSER LOOK: Here's the note from Ilsa that Sam passes along to Rick at the station:

> Richard,
> I cannot go with you or ever see you again.
> You must not ask why.
> Just believe that I love you.
> Go, my darling, and God bless you.
>
> Ilsa

Yikes! For such a short note, this one is a killer. In four short sentences Ilsa covers a lot of ground, and none of it is good for Rick. I'm breaking up with you, you'll never see me again, I can't tell you why it's happening this way; and oh, by the way, I do still love you. With Ilsa's break-up technique leaving much to be desired, she'd better have a good excuse.

CLOSER LOOK: Just to make sure Rick is boarding the right train, we put an eyeball on the departure table for the five o'clock train. Here it is:

DEPART 17 H	
Train 27	**TOUTES CLASSES**
Nuits s/ Ravières	
Dijon, Besançon	
Chalon s/ Saône	
Mâcon	
LYON	
Aix-Les-Bains	
Grenoble	
Briançon	
Valence	
Livron	
Avignon	
MARSEILLE	
Toulon	
NICE	

So all is well—this train is indeed headed to Marseille. The towns posted on the table check out as legitimate stops for trains taking the SNCF Paris-Lyon-Marseille route back in the day. But Rick and Sam better have reserved a sleeping berth. It's a 600-mile milk run to Marseille, so they'll be lucky to pull into Marseille before noon tomorrow.

FILM ANECDOTES: This scene contains the film's best known gaffe. Through most of the scene Rick's raincoat and hat are pretty well soaked. But when Rick boards the train in the final shot his coat and hat look dry. You can definitely see a sheen of water on his left side. Same goes for Sam's coat. But their hats are another story. So to our eye, this is not so much an oversight as a failure to adequately hose down the two actors for the last shot.

RANDOM THOUGHTS: So if you're ever in Paris and want to channel the spirit of Rick and Ilsa's "We'll Always Have Paris" frolic, here's an exhausting itinerary:

Day One:

Morning—Sightseeing along the Seine, including a boat ride past the Eiffel Tower and under Pont Rouelle (snapping a photo at the appropriate spot).

Afternoon—Tour Paris sights by car (open-air roadster optional), including a spin around the Arc de Triomphe, before heading down the Champs-Élysées. Then head east out of Paris to the bucolic Champagne region and Reims. Wind through the vineyards, and catch a tasting at Veuve Clicquot Ponsardin or G.H. Mumm, two houses that produce champagnes featured in *Casablanca*.

Night—Back in Paris for a late dinner and entertainment at Moulin Rouge or Folies Bergère. Then retire to the hotel for some late-night champagne sipping (roaring fire optional).

Day Two:

Morning—A late and extended *petit déjeuner* in a café atop Montmartre.

Afternoon—Explore Montmartre before holing up in a bistro for a bottle (or four) of bubbly.

Night—Gather your things and head for Gare de Lyon to catch an evening train to Marseille, with the option to land in the softer confines of, say, Avignon.

Just be wary if, nearing the end of Day Two, your significant other insists on meeting you at the train station.

Rick's—Main Room

CLOSER LOOK: Going into the flashback, Rick had at least two-fifths of a bottle left. **(38:27)** But after his tortured reminiscence, at least another inch of booze has gone missing, which means he's been drinking as he recalls those heady days in Paris. **(47:56)** One *more* inch and Sam will be carrying Rick up to his apartment.

RANDOM THOUGHTS: It's nice of Sam to stick around and help Rick sort through the mess he's in, but you sure can't blame him for disappearing once Ilsa shows up.

EXPLANATION REQUIRED: Look for the second empty glass on the table. **(48:00)** It's there for a reason. The original script explains that Rick sets an empty glass and chair at the table for Ilsa, anticipating that she'll pay him a late-night visit. In fact, just before the flashback, Rick confesses to Sam that he's expecting a female visitor. Ilsa does take the chair upon arriving, but she declines the drink.

CLOSER LOOK: More inconsistencies creep into this scene. As Rick glares at Ilsa standing in the doorway, he's holding the bourbon bottle in his right hand and a glass in his left. But in the very next shot the bottle and glass have switched places. **(48:22)** Just a minor gaffe involving the table props, so no big deal. But what about the fact that when the flashback started Rick was on the other side of the table, with his back to the front door? **(36:35)** Switching seats mid-flashback is certainly plausible, but it's not what you'd expect.

HISTORY LESSON: Ilsa reveals that she's from Oslo, Norway. Of Germany's invasion targets, Norway came after Austria, Czechoslovakia and Poland. Things had been relatively quiet in the months following Germany's September 1939 taking of Poland, a period known as the Phony War. But on April 9, 1940, Germany got back on the conquering trail by invading Denmark and Norway simultaneously. Denmark wanted no part of it and surrendered immediately. Norway had some fight and managed to hold out until June 9.

CAST ANECDOTES: While Ingrid Bergman plays a woman from Norway's capital, in real life she was from the capital of Norway's next-door neighbor, Sweden. Her segue to America came about through her making of the Swedish film *Intermezzo* (1936). An assistant to Hollywood producer and studio head David O. Selznick screened the film after receiving an elevator-ride tip, and, in turn, recommended to Selznick that he pursue the Swedish starlet. Selznick hooked her on remaking *Intermezzo* in Hollywood, and thus was the beginning of an eight-year run with Selznick.

Bergman's career was distinguished by the broad range of roles she tackled. To see her play opposite ends of the purity spectrum with equal proficiency, watch *Dr. Jekyll and Mr. Hyde* (1941), in which she plays a barmaid and sometime prostitute, and *The Bells of St. Mary's* (1945), in which she plays a nun.

JUST WONDERING: Knowing now that Rick left Paris with no game plan and virtually nothing to his name, how exactly has Rick managed to gain such prominence in Casablanca, and so quickly? Rick left Paris for Marseille in mid-June 1940. By December 1941, he heads the hottest joint in Casablanca, and practically owns the town. Just where did he get the funds, and the connections for that matter, required to succeed in the ever-corrupt Casablanca?

CHAPTER 5

THE BLACK MARKET

"If I could lay my hands on those letters, I could make a fortune."
— Signor Ferrari

Day two in Casablanca kicks off with the mid-morning meeting in Captain Renault's office that Major Strasser insisted upon last night. There, Strasser and Renault advise Victor that, as an escaped prisoner of the Reich, he is not eligible for an exit visa. Still, Strasser dangles the offer of uninhibited passage out of Casablanca—all Victor has to do is provide the names of fellow Resistance leaders.

The offer gives Victor the perfect opportunity to sound off on Strasser, explaining why the Nazis will never prevail. Renault and Strasser counter with a classic intimidation tactic. First Renault explains that Ugarte, the man with whom Victor sought to connect with last night, is dead. Then Renault and Strasser imply that Ugarte died at the hands of the authorities. The unmistakable message to Victor? Pursuing the letters of transit will not be good for his health.

Well, Renault predicts that Victor will end up in the black market in search of exit visas, and sure enough that is where we head next. In the heart of the black market sits Ferrari's bar, the Blue Parrot. Rick pays Ferrari a visit, and before long Ferrari cagily offers to front the sale of the letters of transit.

During Ferrari's proposition, Rick spots Ilsa outside browsing the market. Rick heads out, breezing past Victor at the door, and is soon sharing a discreet word with Ilsa. He starts by apologizing for his bourbon-induced rants the night before, but quickly presses Ilsa for answers. Why did she leave him? Why is she here now? Ilsa declines to respond.

But Rick's soul-searching over the last year and a half has him convinced that Ilsa dumped him because it was too dangerous to hang out with someone wanted by the Nazis. Upon floating this theory to Ilsa, Rick regains some of the swagger he displayed in Paris, and all but dares Ilsa to stop by his apartment for a more private moment. With Rick headed down an amorous path, Ilsa feels she must come clean. And it's a three-part shocker: she's married, she's married to Victor Laszlo and she's been married to Victor Laszlo since before she and Rick were together in Paris. Ouch.

Back inside the Blue Parrot, Victor and Ilsa reconnect and approach Ferrari about acquiring two exit visas. Given Victor's predicament, Ferrari is too smart to consider selling him an exit visa; but he is willing to sell one to Ilsa. Victor and Ilsa mull it over, and decide that it's two exit visas or none. But before they go, Ferrari offers Victor an intriguing tip. The letters of transit that Victor was supposed to buy from Ugarte? They are, most likely, in Rick's possession. For Victor, this guy Rick just won't go away.

Captain Renault's Office

CLOSER LOOK: We barely have time to pull up a chair in Captain Renault's office before another gaffe comes to light. Peering into the office through a window, we see Renault standing in front of a large map. Plenty of shadows are cast upon the map, but none from the blades of a rotating ceiling fan, right? But in the next shot the map is awash in fan-generated shadows. Now how hard can it be to remember to keep the ceiling fan on for the entire day's shooting?

HISTORY LESSON: According to Renault, he was with the Americans when they "blundered" into Berlin in 1918. If he means to imply that there was a post-war American military presence in Berlin, that never happened. Now the Allies did occupy the Rhineland, and American troops advanced as far east as the Rhine River, but that's about it. No long march to Berlin. So while Renault was in the trenches during the war, he seems to have forgotten how the thing ended.

CAST ANECDOTES: Actor Claude Rains, like his character in *Casablanca*, was a World War I veteran. But Rains served for the Brits, whereas Renault served for France. Rains belonged to a British regiment called the "London Scottish," and fought near a notorious section of the Western Front known as Vimy Ridge. In September 1914, the Germans took the high ground at Vimy Ridge and didn't relinquish it for more than two and a half years. In March 1916, the British relieved the beleaguered French from this area of the front, with Rains' regiment showing up later that summer. Unfortunately, Rains and his mates had an equally tough go of it. It took until April 1917 for the Allies to finally knock the Germans off Vimy Ridge, and it wasn't the Brits or French who did it but rather some plucky Canadian forces utilizing fresh military tactics.

During combat Rains had the misfortune of being exposed to a gas attack, with long-term effects. Both sides resorted to chemical warfare throughout the war, using tear gas early on before graduating to more insidious gases with lethal properties, such as chlorine, phosgene and mustard gas. Rains is said to have been exposed to mustard gas, which the Germans began using in 1917. While he apparently escaped any permanent physical scarring (mustard gas is a blistering agent), he did lose sight in his right eye. It therefore makes sense that in *Passage to Marseille* Rains, playing a World War I veteran, wears a patch over his right eye. We looked for evidence of Rains favoring his left side in *Casablanca*, but he hides the disability nicely.

Discharged with the rank of captain (same as Renault), Rains soon took to theater. As early as 1926 you could have caught him on Broadway. By 1933 he was appearing in American films, and by 1938 he was a U.S. citizen.

JUST WONDERING: Why does Renault say to Strasser that he should be interested to know that Victor is headed over to Renault's office? Strasser called for the meeting last night, insisting that Victor and Ilsa meet him in Renault's office at 10:00 a.m. sharp.

CLOSER LOOK: Outside Renault's office, Victor and Ilsa cross paths with the other couple seeking exits visas in this film, Jan and Annina Brandel. Our view of the action in the lobby is all too brief, plus the signs are hard to read, but here's an overview. Above the entrance is a sign that reads Service—Passports and Visas—3rd Door (*Service–Passeports et Visas–3rd Porte*). Inside are signs for three queues (only the first one is legible): Authorization to Stay (*Permis de Séjour*), Visas for French People (*Visas pour les Français*) and Visas to Leave (*Visas de Sortie*). Jan and Annina Brandel are in this last queue and having no luck convincing the clerk to issue them exit visas.

On the wall is a sign reading Secretary—Prefect's Office (*Secrétariat–Bureau du Préfet*). Another indicates that the criminal investigations office (*Police Judiciaire*) and archives are upstairs. The building directory outside the Préfecture de Police, which we detailed earlier, lists both offices as being upstairs, so a nice, if obscure, consistency here.

DID YOU KNOW?: In real life, instead of trekking to Casablanca, any refugee stuck in France would have been wise to track down one of two men, Varian Fry or Aristides de Sousa Mendes. Both were angels of sorts, and responsible for saving thousands of lives.

Varian Fry was an American who traveled to Marseille after the fall of France on a mission to help political and intellectual refugees escape from France. Many of his clients were public figures and already on the Gestapo's blacklist, so the threat of being caught and thrown in a concentration camp was real and imminent. Fry prioritized cases based on a refugee's political, cultural and intellectual prominence. Victor's background would have landed him at the top of Fry's client list; plus, and as we learn later in the film, Victor was conveniently in Marseille just before he went to Casablanca.

Fry's objective was to secure the requisite travel papers, real or forged, to enable the client to leave France for good. No escape gambit or route was discounted, and Fry even made use of the circuitous Oran–Casablanca–Lisbon route. However, his main strategy was to smuggle refugees over the southernmost part of the French-Spanish frontier via established escape trails leading to Lisbon. Refugees had to avoid French border patrols, and their transit papers had to pass muster with Spanish border officials. And you risked prison time in Spain if you traveled beyond the border area without first presenting yourself to Spanish border officials. In one year (before Vichy authorities finally got wise and deported him) Fry arranged for the safe passage of more than 1,500 refugees.

If you want to hike Fry's preferred France-Spain border crossing route, go to Cerbère, France, a seaside town right on the France-Spain border. Head up through the cemetery, find the trail up to the top of the hill, then drop down the other side into Spain and the town of Portbou. It's a pleasant hike, with moderate terrain and great views, all of which belies the fear refugees must have experienced taking the very same path. Imagine how it must have felt to crest the hill and take those first steps into Spain, knowing there was no turning back.

In contrast to Fry, Sousa Mendes' work benefited common refugees like Jan and Annina Brandel. In May 1940, Sousa Mendes was the Portuguese consul-general in Bordeaux, France. Refugees trying to outrun the German army streamed into Bordeaux and other cities on the French-Spanish border. In a stroke of genius, Sousa Mendes hit on the idea of issuing Portuguese visas to refugees en masse out of the Portuguese consulates in Bordeaux, Toulouse, Hendaye and Bayonne. He did this despite the fact that several months earlier the Portuguese government had forbidden the practice. The government eventually put a stop to Sousa Mendes' disobedience, but by then Sousa Mendes had had an extraordinary impact. In just a few frenetic weeks he managed to issue visas for an astounding 30,000 refugees.

To learn more about the remarkable wartime achievements of these two men, track down *Surrender on Demand* by Fry and *A Good Man in Evil Times* by José-Alain Fralon.

JUST WONDERING: Since when have the Germans become so accommodating in pursuing enemies of the Reich, particularly one with Victor's track record? Victor is not only a German war criminal on account of his Resistance activities, but he's also an *escaped prisoner.* Does it really matter that he is technically standing in unoccupied France? If anything, that cuts in favor of the Germans arresting him on the spot. Heck, the Germans just conquered France and permitted a collaborationist French government to oversee unoccupied French territories. What good is it having a puppet government if you're not pulling the strings?

RANDOM THOUGHTS: Strasser tells Victor he can leave for Lisbon upon providing the names and whereabouts of the leaders of the Resistance in the following European cities: Paris, Prague, Brussels, Amsterdam, Oslo, Belgrade and Athens. All are capital cities in countries occupied by Germany. If we're talking German occupation or Axis membership, he could also have thrown in Vienna, Copenhagen, Warsaw, Sofia, Bucharest, and Luxembourg City among others.

HISTORY LESSON: We know the hands-off treatment received by Victor is implausible, but there's actually a practical reason why things would not have gone down this way. The armistice France signed with Germany in June 1940 contained an article that required France to "surrender upon demand all Germans" to be found in France. At first blush Article 19, as it is notoriously known, seems to simply allow the repatriation of wayward Germans lost in the war's shuffle. But make no mistake, Article 19's intent was insidious. The Germans used it to facilitate recapturing enemies of the Reich—cultural, racial, political or otherwise—who had managed to slip into French territories.

Germans, you see, encompassed any citizen of any country already sacked by Germany, such as Poland, Austria, Hungary and Victor's homeland, Czechoslovakia. And *France* included "French possessions, colonies, protectorate territories and mandates." This means that, as a Czechoslovakian hanging out in the French protectorate of Morocco, Victor was Article 19 material all the way. Indeed, that's why last night, when Victor told Strasser that he's a Czechoslovakian, Strasser quickly corrected him that he *was* a Czechoslovakian but now is a subject of the Reich. **(28:10)**

FILM ANECDOTES: Notice the curious white or grey streak in Victor's hair throughout the film. This detail was the producer's idea, designed to show that Victor's time in a German concentration camp had taken its toll. Also contributing to that impression is a nasty scar above Victor's right eye, perhaps received from a prison guard.

JUST WONDERING: How did Renault know, as he claims, that last night Victor was inquiring about Ugarte? Victor never mentioned Ugarte in Renault's presence. Now, Renault's men could have choked it out of Ugarte before they finished him off. Or they could have forced a confession out of Resistance member Berger. But our theory is that Renault was bluffing, and Victor unwittingly conceded something that Renault suspected, but didn't actually know.

RANDOM THOUGHTS: As the meeting wraps up, one of Renault's assistants enters the room and explains that, "another visa problem has come up." Renault instructs him to "show her in," and eagerly prepares for the encounter. It's clear from the exchange that Renault has worked this angle before. And given that we just saw Jan and Annina outside Renault's office getting rejected in their bid for visas, it's a fair bet that Annina is the woman who is about to step into Renault's den.

CAST ANECDOTES: Henreid plays a Czechoslovakian in the film. He was in fact born in 1908 in Austria-Hungary, which at that time included the land that later became Czechoslovakia. As an adult Henreid lived in Vienna, placing him squarely within the Nazi sphere of terror. And while he was never really in peril he did have plenty to worry about. His wife had Jewish heritage, plus life in Vienna under Nazi rule was harsh, and his mother refused to leave the city.

Henreid had a brush with the Nazis in the mid-1930s after Germany's largest film studio extended him a contract offer. As told by Henreid, he turned it down upon discovering that the offer came with strings attached— he would have to sign papers acknowledging Nazi party allegiance.

In 1938, Henreid left Vienna, a decision that was influenced as much by career aspirations as safety considerations. Henreid leveraged his growing reputation in Vienna's theater scene to land stage work in London. While he viewed film acting as somewhat beneath his talents, he still saw fit to jump on prominent roles in two British film hits, *Goodbye, Mr. Chips* (1939) and *Night Train* (1940). Hollywood took notice and lured Henreid further away from the stage.

But before he could get to Hollywood, just *staying* in Great Britain was no small trick. Henreid, you see, was technically the enemy. That's because when Germany sacked Austria in the March 1938 Anschluss, the Nazis forced German citizenship on all Austrians. The Allies, ever fearful of enemy infiltrations through emigration, were not in the mood to disagree.

The upshot? In the eyes of the British government Henreid was an enemy alien, and therefore subject to internment. He managed to avoid this fate through some fast talking and a few key character witnesses, including, word has it, fellow *Casablanca* actor Conrad Veidt. According to Henreid, the U.S. denied his application for a visa because he was Austrian, but he then convinced the American consulate to grant him entry under the Italian quota. Apparently, this smooth move turned on the argument that he was technically Italian since he was born in Trieste, Austria-Hungary and Trieste had become part of Italy in 1920.

However it happened, on August 12, 1940, Henreid and his wife landed in New York, accompanied by their pet terrier and 2,000 British pounds—then worth $8,000 U.S. dollars—stashed behind a mirror. That's a good-sized starter kit—$8,000 in 1940 is equivalent to around $143,000 today—and quite a bit more than the pocket change Marcel Dalio and Madeleine LeBeau had when they arrived a few weeks later.

CLOSER LOOK: Notice the elaborate wall map of Morocco in Renault's office. Drafted in French, the map identifies several of the larger Moroccan cities, including, naturally, Casablanca. More interestingly, we have seen this map before. At the beginning of the film, when a local official reads an all-points bulletin regarding the murder of two German couriers, a wall map of Morocco is visible in the background. And it's the same one that appears in Renault's office.

The Black Market

CLOSER LOOK: Mixing things up a bit, we head over to the Blue Parrot—Rick's main competition—to see how Casablanca's daytime barflies are getting along. The establishing shot for the scene shows a market bursting with activity. **(54:40)** Closer scrutiny of the shot confirms that this is the same set used for the earlier scene where a crowd gathered in front of the Préfecture de Police watches Strasser's plane fly overhead.

The main giveaways are some minor set features that appear in the Préfecture de Police scene as well—a streetlamp, a store sign for the perfume shop Kiss of the Desert, and, farther up the street, a poster. The set designers used wooden awnings in this scene but not in the earlier one, and this is clearly supposed to be the black market, not the exterior of the Préfecture de Police. We know the crew was working on a shoestring film budget, but double-dipping on a set definitely qualifies as a film gaffe.

FILM ANECDOTES: This scene also makes use of matte paintings to fill in the scene, mostly for the upper buildings and the sky. If matte paintings weren't used here, you'd be looking beyond the walls of the Warner Bros. studio lot and onto the streets of Burbank, California.

EXPLANATION REQUIRED: In an earlier scene, the one in which a crowd watches Strasser's plane overhead, we pointed out that several people held booklets, and identified the booklets as France-issued passports. This scene provides the clue that enabled us to make that call. The cover of the passport shown here matches up with the covers of the booklets shown in the earlier scene. **(54:45)**

The cover also matches up with French passports from the pre-World War II era. On the cover is a French emblem—the center features the letters R and F interlocking, standing for *République Française*. Below the emblem are spaces (top to bottom) for the passport number, the holder's last name and the holder's first name. Given the timing, these really should be Vichy-issued passports, but we're guessing they were not exactly handy for prop team reference.

The Blue Parrot

DID YOU KNOW?: Well, it's not called the Blue Parrot for nothing, and as you might expect there are a few parrots to be found in the place. Indeed, a rather impressive one is perched at the front door. So is there actually a blue parrot species? Of some three-hundred thirty species of parrot worldwide, dozens have *blue* in the name—blue-winged, blue-throated and blue-headed, blue-rumped, blue-fronted...you get the picture. But none goes simply by blue parrot.

So what type of parrot is the fellow at the door? Well, he's definitely a macaw, and of those a scarlet macaw best fits the, er, bill. The parrot's large size, white cheek patches and light-colored bill are all giveaways. The macaw's red, blue and yellow plumage is striking, but this is black and white *Casablanca*, not Technicolor *Wizard of Oz*, so you'll have to use your imagination.

CLOSER LOOK: While Ferrari chose to use English for the establishment's main sign, he has not forgotten his French-speaking patrons. Beneath the overhang you can just make out the Blue Parrot's French equivalent, *Perroquet Bleu*. **(54:59)**

EXPLANATION REQUIRED: Also greeting patrons at the entrance is an Arabic symbol known as a hamsa—a hand with five fingers. Look for it on the wall to the left of the front door, just under the parrot. **(54:59)** A little later, beneath the hamsa you can see writing in Arabic, which legitimately translates to *Blue Parrot*. **(56:33)**

The hamsa, also called the Hand of Fatima, is believed to have talisman powers, and is often displayed on walls in the hopes of keeping evil at bay. And it appears to be working—no sign of Strasser in the Blue Parrot. Perhaps Rick should look into hanging a hamsa of his own.

CLOSER LOOK: Inside the bar more parrots lurk. One can be spied as Rick walks across the bar the first time. **(55:08)** There's also a stuffed parrot in a case on the wall behind Rick when he sits down with Ferrari. **(55:35)** And a few scenes down the road a ceramic parrot (wings spread) rests on Ferrari's desk. **(1:31:33)**

And then there's the ominous "shadow" parrot. As Ferrari, Ilsa and Victor wrap up their conversation, in three successive shots the eerie shadow of a perched parrot looms behind Ferrari. On quick glance the shadow doesn't seem real. But look closely at the first shot—the bird's head definitely moves. **(1:00:21)**

CLOSER LOOK: Besides parrots, there are lots of interesting things to see in the Blue Parrot. Hookahs abound, folks play cards and sip coffee, local and foreign officers mingle, and every gent seems to have a female companion or two. In a corner, some musicians (including a flutist) play for a woman performing the lost art of shadow dancing. Look for her (and her shadow) in the background when Rick first walks into the bar **(55:01)**, again when Rick stands talking to Ferrari **(55:30)**, and a third time as Rick heads out the door. **(56:38)**

RANDOM THOUGHTS: Rick remarks to Ferrari that the bus is in, so he'll take his shipment now. Indeed, the bus really is in—we just saw it pull into the market in the establishing shot. **(54:40)** Signage on the back, in French, confirms that it's a Moroccan transport company. One lucky extra got the plumb assignment of riding atop the bus with a dog. No word here on exactly what comprises Rick's shipment (though later on we do get a clue). Despite his commercial successes, Rick still hasn't learned how to get around Casablanca's leading middleman. It seems that all roads to profit run through Ferrari.

RANDOM THOUGHTS: Ferrari's discussions with Rick prove yet again that in Casablanca shadiness and professionalism are not at all conflicting qualities. Indeed, Ferrari pretty well sums it up when he declares, in all seriousness, that being the head of Casablanca's black-market activities makes him a man of influence and respect.

CAST ANECDOTES: Behind Ferrari's unapologetic and forthright approach to black marketeering is actor Sydney Greenstreet. Born in 1879 in the coastal town of Sandwich, England (due west of London), Greenstreet spent four contented decades on stage in England and America before making his first feature film in 1941.

Greenstreet specialized in works of Shakespeare, and if you had been in New York way back in 1907 you could have seen him make his Broadway debut in *The Merchant of Venice*. During World War I, with things more than a little unsettled in Europe, he made regular appearances on Broadway. In 1932, he crossed paths with fellow *Casablanca* actor Claude Rains in a successful Broadway adaptation of Pearl S. Buck's *The Good Earth*, with Greenstreet playing the despicable uncle of Rains' protagonist character.

At the age of 61, Greenstreet finally got around to filmmaking. His introduction to Hollywood could not have gone much better. In his first film he appeared with Bogart and Lorre in *The Maltese Falcon*, and gained an Academy Award nomination for Best Supporting Actor. Three pictures later he reunited with Bogart and Lorre in *Casablanca*. So that's two American classics out of just four pictures. Not bad.

The Maltese Falcon established Greenstreet and Lorre as a powerful film duo. Of some two dozen films to his credit, Greenstreet shared nine with Lorre (including one in which they played themselves). Interestingly, while producers and directors sought the pair for their obvious chemistry, in *Casablanca* they don't share a scene together. Ferrari is in Rick's Café the night of Ugarte's arrest, but their paths never cross. Too bad, as an exchange between these two black market brokers over the whereabouts of the letters of transit would have been a delight to watch. To see Greenstreet and Lorre enjoy some quality screen time together, check out *The Mask of Dimitrios* (1944). To see Greenstreet tackle a comedy with equal skill, watch *Christmas in Connecticut* (1945).

CLOSER LOOK: Some inconsistencies appear in this scene involving the bottle of liquor ordered by Ferrari. A waiter delivers the bottle, and Ferrari uncorks it, pours himself a drink and replaces the cork. **(56:12)** A few seconds later the bottle disappears. **(56:15)** A few more seconds and the cork has magically freed itself and rests aside the bottle. **(56:23)** While the disappearing bottle could be blocked by Ferrari's shoulder, we think not. In previous shots with identical framing, the top of the bottle is at least as high as Rick's lapel notch. Even with Ferrari's rotund frame in the mix, the bottle's neck should be visible.

DID YOU KNOW?: Bourbon isn't the only thing being quaffed at the Blue Parrot. Several patrons are drinking Turkish coffee. Look for the waiter serving the coffee at a table just before Rick and Ferrari sit down. We know that it's Turkish coffee by the small odd-shaped pot called a cezve and the demitasse cups. Larger on the bottom and narrower at the top, the cezve causes water to boil up through very fine grounds. The result is a rich, powerful concoction that is sure to catapult you through the day. A cezve and demitasse cups are also visible when Rick calls on Ferrari the second time, and at Rick's when Carl serves a table of gamblers. **(8:24)**

JUST WONDERING: How was Rick able to sit through Ferrari drinking bourbon without getting the slightest bit queasy, given that he practically passed out on the stuff just last night? We know it's still morning because Rick tells Ferrari he doesn't drink before noon, plus Victor bids Rick "good morning" at the door. And we know it's the same liquor Rick had last night because the bottle labels match. The brand is Kentucky Hill, and the label reads Kentucky Straight Bourbon Whiskey. **(49:20; 56:28)** True to his word, Rick does not drink with Ferrari. When Rick gets up to leave you can see that his shot glass is still upside down. **(56:29)**

FILM ANECDOTES: We spied this same Bourbon Hill bottle label in another Warner Bros. film, *Mildred Pierce* (1945). Look for it as the amorous Wally Fay (Jack Carson) pours a drink for himself and Mildred (Joan Crawford).

The Black Market

EXPLANATION REQUIRED: While meeting with Ferrari, Rick sees Ilsa and Victor in a shop across the way. Two shop signs are visible, one in French, the other in Arabic. The French sign reads *Au Roi de la Lingerie*, which translates to, The King of Underclothes. Hmmm. That doesn't sound right. The prop team probably intended to refer to "linens"—Rick and Ilsa do browse some table linens, and *lingerie* does have history as an old French term for linen goods. Anyway, the sign in Arabic translates to, King of the Silk. Unfortunately, in wartime Casablanca, there would not be much silk to reign over.

RANDOM THOUGHTS: Ilsa's large-brimmed sun hat is a very practical choice for a day in the hot Casablanca sun, though it's not exactly travel-friendly given her current situation. It's hard to see, but a thin ribbon encircling the crown ends in a bow in the back and is adorned with a few pearls. We love this hat for its mix of style and function, but overall the ensemble seems a bit formal for a trip to the market.

CAST ANECDOTES: The haggling merchant scene is one of the script's few missteps. The bartering gag is forced and gets in the way of Bogart and Bergman's serious exchange. Plus, actor Frank Puglia, who was born in Sicily and no doubt cast for his plausibly local looks, is not all that convincing as a Berber merchant. Certainly his made up accent and fake beard do not help things, but the real problem is that Puglia is asked to play the scene as if he's in a Marx Brothers film, mugging for the camera throughout. You get the sense that Bogart and Bergman are wincing inside as he delivers his lines. Interestingly, post-production Hal Wallis ordered the gag's deletion, retaining only the merchant's initial reference to 700 francs and his parting line. But the producer did not follow his instincts, and the gag made the cut.

CLOSER LOOK: In the Blue Parrot, notice that Ilsa takes off her gloves before accepting a beverage from Ferrari. Indeed, proper glove etiquette calls for their removal before handling food or drink. And when she's finished and set to leave the Blue Parrot she puts them back on. Further evidence that Ilsa is all class.

RANDOM THOUGHTS: Ilsa mentions here two French cities that she and Victor passed through during the war—Lille and Marseille. These cities are quite far apart. Lille is in northernmost France; Marseille is in southern France on the Mediterranean coast.

Of these two wartime stops, the first one doesn't make much sense. At the beginning of the Battle of France, Lille had the misfortune of being squarely in the path of the German army's initial *blitzkrieg*. In late May 1940, Lille fell into German hands. So when Victor and Ilsa reconnected in Paris in June 1940 (as we learn later), Lille was already behind enemy lines, and it would have been foolish for them to go there for any reason.

And Ilsa does not seem to be referring to time together in Lille before the Battle of France. Ilsa mentions having trouble getting out of Lille, and this would only have been a challenge starting in mid-May 1940 when the Battle of France kicked off. So the timing doesn't work with them reconnecting just a few weeks later in Paris—in May Victor surely was either in a concentration camp or had just escaped.

Their stopover in Marseille does make sense. Marseille, due to its location and size, was a natural gathering point and crossroads for refugees. In fact, they could have saved themselves the trouble of traveling to Casablanca had they spent some time tracking down forged travel papers there. With a decent amount of money, aid from a Varian Fry-type and a little luck, they could have made it across the border to Spain and been in Lisbon in a matter of weeks.

RANDOM THOUGHTS: The all-knowing Ferrari—at least when it comes to illegal activities—tips Victor off to the fact that he's being trailed. Victor says he already knows it. Maybe so, but *we* don't. Just to make sure we didn't miss something, we combed the market scenes for someone trailing the couple. But unless it's the haggling merchant we can't find the shadow.

CLOSER LOOK: After Ferrari instructs his headwaiter not to do *something* for more than fifty francs, watch Ferrari sneak back the house flyswatter from the headwaiter. **(1:00:05)** Apparently, flies are a big problem at the Blue Parrot. Fly strips are everywhere. And Ferrari has become an expert fly swatter over the years. He delivers two fatal swats in the film, one here just after Victor and Ilsa leave **(1:01:05)** and one the next day when Rick calls on Ferrari. **(1:32:06)**

FILM ANECDOTES: With *Casablanca* incorporating just a scattershot collection of lines from the play, the overall depth of the dialogue is squarely attributable to the film's writers, Julius and Philip Epstein and Howard Koch. And Warner Bros. veteran Casey Robinson also was in the mix for a spell, though uncredited.

The debate over who did what and when is well documented, and long ago proved to be maddeningly unsolvable. However things went down, the writers were at their best in a high-pressure situation that found them delivering scenes just ahead of the daily shoots. Despite differing styles, and Koch and the brothers working in separate corners, they managed to corral the various plotlines and heady political ideas ricocheting through the film into a smart, yet, relatable story. And somehow they found a way to blend in healthy doses of cynicism and snark without overpowering the messages of optimism and resolve. It all added up to a much-deserved Academy Award for Best Adapted Screenplay.

The Epstein brothers were a true team, which makes sense given they were identical twins. They had only been collaborating on screenplays for a few years before taking on *Casablanca*. And the assignment was no accident. Jack Warner knew *Casablanca* needed special attention, and the two were masters at taking serviceable material and whipping into it depth and substance and wit and humor.

Julius explained that the two always worked together as if they were one person, and tackled scenes together, never separately. Well, they certainly put that approach to good use on *Casablanca*. As filming hurtled toward a wrap, the ending still had not been written. Ingrid Bergman didn't even know how to play Ilsa as it was unclear who she would end up with. With everyone feeling the pressure from Jack Warner, the brothers simultaneously brainstormed the last scene's "round of the usual suspects" resolution while driving into the studio one day. Given how much guff the two had taken from Jack Warner over the years for not keeping normal business hours at the studio, it's only fitting that they were "off the clock" at the time.

Interestingly, Julius viewed *Casablanca* through the prism of formulaic Hollywood filmmaking, and through the years described it in interviews as "slick" and lacking reality. Even in private moments, his take was pragmatic: Philip Epstein's grandson is Major League Baseball executive Theo Epstein, and as a child Theo similarly recalled his granduncle Julius telling him that *Casablanca* was the same old Hollywood stuff.

Well, it's certainly fair to say that *Casablanca* leans heavily on Hollywood formulas, but we say Julius was being more than a bit modest. Even formulas can produce film magic.

As for Koch, beyond *Casablanca* his writing skills were famously displayed in a 1938 radio play adaptation of Orson Wells' novel "The War of the Worlds." Between the writing and the acting, the show sounded so realistic that many listeners thought Martians really were coming to get us. Some might say his writing on that project was, um, otherworldly.

CHAPTER 6

THE NIGHT IN CASABLANCA HEATS UP

"If Laszlo's presence in a café can inspire this unfortunate demonstration, what more will his presence in Casablanca bring on?"
— Major Strasser

It's our second night in Casablanca, and with all the excitement last night at Rick's we absolutely have to go back. But at once we sense that trouble is afoot. The place is honeycombed with German officers, and straightaway a fight breaks out at the bar over Yvonne having taken up company with one of them. Emotions are running high tonight.

Just as things settle down, Victor and Ilsa make an encore appearance. Rick is in no mood for another run-in with Ilsa, but there's not much he can do about it. Overnight, sorrow has turned to bitterness, and he can't resist the petty gesture of having Sam play their once-favorite song.

Rick tries to take his mind off things with a drink, but soon is interrupted by Annina, the refugee from Bulgaria. She and her husband are still desperate for exit visas, and Captain Renault has her contemplating trading visas for a one-time tryst. At first Rick shows little sympathy for her predicament, but later he heads to the gambling room intent on thwarting Renault's gambit. Annina's husband is losing big at roulette until Rick gives him a betting tip. With two spins of the wheel the couple has enough money for exit visas, and Annina can sidestep Renault's lecherous proposition.

Meanwhile, back in the main room Victor wants a word with Rick. Armed with Ferrari's tip that Rick may have the letters of transit, Victor implores Rick to sell them to him. Victor appeals to Rick's patriotism and penchant for aiding the underdog, but Rick isn't biting. No amount of money is going to convince him to sell those letters to Victor.

This makes little sense to Victor. If *anything* talks in Casablanca, it's money. Rick explains that if he wants the full rationale, he'll have to ask his wife. Victor is taken aback by Rick's remark, but before he can probe further another skirmish erupts in the main room.

This time, the Germans taunt the Free France loyalists by singing a German war anthem. When Victor leads the loyalists in an in-kind response, Major Strasser is not amused. So in classic Third Reich fashion Strasser regains control of the situation through a show of power. First, he orders Renault to shut down the Café. Then he tracks down Ilsa to deliver a sobering message: there are three scenarios under which Victor might leave Casablanca, and none of them end well for Victor.

While everyone else, no doubt, heads over to the Blue Parrot, we are stuck following Victor and Ilsa back to their hotel room. Victor is intent on going to the Resistance meeting that Berger invited him to last night, but matters of love and fidelity are also weighing on his mind. Victor has added up all of Rick and Ilsa's offhand remarks and has a pretty good idea that the two have some history. But, ever the gentleman, he does not confront Ilsa so much as give her the opportunity to confess. When Ilsa throws around a bunch of non-committal doubletalk, Victor starts looking like the odd man out in this love triangle.

Indeed, just after Victor leaves for his meeting, Ilsa slips out of the hotel herself. Over at the Café, Rick and Carl assess how long they can afford to keep the doors closed. In time, Rick heads up to his apartment, where he gets quite a shock: Ilsa lying in wait.

But this is not the social call Rick envisioned earlier in the black market. Ilsa has only one thing on her mind ...the letters of transit. Rick is having none of it, and reaches into his cynical core for more sharp remarks. Ilsa first tries to reason with Rick, then makes an emotional plea, and finally tries to shame him into submission with a barrage of insults. Rick diffuses each ploy with little trouble.

Left with no other options, Ilsa turns to sheer force and brandishes a pistol. But Rick knows that she lacks the resolve to follow through, and the weapon quickly gives way to tears. The two embrace in a wondrous kiss, and the rest is left to our imagination.

In time Ilsa explains how this whole mess came to be. Her story seems to hold up. Ilsa has been a tough read so far on the love front, but she makes it pretty clear here that she's still in love with Rick. This is now officially a complicated mess, and one that requires much thinking. And when Ilsa tells Rick that he will have to think for them both, Rick takes it to heart.

This long and exhausting day has one more episode. Victor and Carl, who have been at a Resistance meeting, find themselves being chased by gendarmes. They appear to slip the authorities by ducking into a side entrance to the Café. Alas, this creates a new problem—Victor is now in the main room and his wife is still upstairs in Rick's apartment. Rick deftly calls on Carl to sneak Ilsa out the back door. With that sticky situation resolved, Rick steps in to help Victor tend to a small wound incurred while fleeing the gendarmes. Along the way, the two touch on political ideology, Ilsa Lund, the letters of transit and destiny. But their discussion is cut short when the pursuing gendarmes circle back, storm the Café and arrest Victor.

Rick's—Main Room

RANDOM THOUGHTS: At the bar, Casablanca's resident pickpocket separates another gentleman from his wallet, before bumping into an understandably paranoid Carl. The lesson here? Never trust an amusing little fellow in a bow tie, sporting a bamboo cane and wearing a pith helmet in a nightclub.

CAST ANECDOTES: Playing the nimble-fingered pickpocket is Berlin native Curt Bois. Bois was among the scores of Jewish actors who fled Germany just after Hitler came to power in 1933, recognizing that it was just a matter of time before they would be banned from film and subject to persecution. Bois was an established comedic film star in Germany before being pushed off screen, with several leading roles to his credit. He left Vienna for New York in late 1934, spent a few tough years on stage in Broadway productions, and debuted in American film in 1937. There he resumed his comedic ways, but the starring roles were no more and Bois adjusted to making the most of bit parts.

Bois stuck around Hollywood for a few years after the war, but in 1950 he had the urge to return to his hometown of Berlin. Only now he had to choose between East and West Berlin. He chose the former, but when the communist-run film scene didn't quite pan out he found his way to the other side of the Wall.

It took him a while to win back audiences, put off by his initial decision to go East, but he flourished for another three-plus decades. All told, with Bois having started his career in 1907 as one of film's original child actors, his career spanned a staggering eighty years.

If you want to see more of Bois track down *The Hunchback of Notre Dame* (1939), *The Amazing Dr. Clitterhouse* (1938, with Bogart) and *Saratoga Trunk* (1945, with Ingrid Bergman).

FILM ANECDOTES: Bois was originally slated to play Carl, but apparently a thin headwaiter wouldn't do, and the part went to the ample S.Z. Sakall. Early production materials described Bois' pickpocket character as a "dark European." Later Warner Bros. identified the petty thief as Italian on the logic that it did not want to offend audiences abroad, and the easy fix was to associate unseemly characters with an Axis country. Of course, such hand-wringing made no sense given that the pickpocket's homeland is never mentioned.

MUSIC NOTES: Strasser arrives this evening as the house orchestra plays an instrumental, which is actually a blending of two songs. First, Señorita Andreya greets the German entourage with "If I Could Be with You (One Hour Tonight)." Take time, once again, to admire her phantom guitar-strumming. **(1:01:34)** Jazz piano great James P. Johnson, the Father of Stride Piano, penned this melody in 1926. Louis Armstrong brought it mainstream in 1930. The song, which includes a nifty muted-trumpet solo, lasts through Renault joining Rick at his table. Originally Sam was slated to sing here, but somewhere along the way the idea got dropped.

The second song, "You Must Have Been a Beautiful Baby," starts with a trombone solo just as Yvonne enters the room. A fitting tribute to Yvonne's natural beauty we suppose. This one was written by the team of Harry Warren and Johnny Mercer for the 1938 Warner Bros. romantic comedy *Hard to Get*. At the time Warren was the lead composer at Warner Bros. Later in 1938 the song topped the charts thanks to Bing Crosby.

CLOSER LOOK: And now for a second look at Strasser's uniform. Centered on Strasser's left breast pocket is an Iron Cross. The fact that it's a pin and not a ribbon tells us Strasser has earned a "First Class" Iron Cross. Impressive. Below the Iron Cross is a Luftwaffe Pilot's Badge—an eagle clutching a swastika, encircled by an oak and laurel wreath.

But there's more to Strasser's military garb than just medals and badges. Zero in on Strasser's left leg as he enters the Café and you'll find a dagger hanging off of his belt. **(1:01:28)** It's a ceremonial dagger worn by Luftwaffe officers. You can see it in most scenes he's in, though it's always hard to spy. Let's hope that tonight the dagger stays in its scabbard.

CLOSER LOOK: A quick time out here to examine an extended gaffe involving Rick and a bottle of cognac. It starts with Carl hustling over to Rick's table with a near-full bottle. **(1:01:45)** When Renault joins Rick a few seconds later, suddenly the bottle is only half full. **(1:01:51)** Now, we know Rick is a professional drinker, but he's not *that* good. Rick then grabs a glass for Renault off a nearby tray. A few seconds earlier there were three glasses on the tray, now there are four. Finally, by the time Annina stops over the bottle is full again and the glass tray is gone. **(1:04:58)**

RANDOM THOUGHTS: While champagne certainly flows freely throughout *Casablanca*, there's plenty of brandy being poured as well. In addition to this one, several scenes in the Café feature folks ordering or downing brandy (oftentimes cognac), including Ugarte in the gambling room, Rick and Renault on the terrace, Rick and Renault in Rick's office, Rick and Carl at the bar after Rick saves Annina from Renault, Victor and Ilsa at their table on the second night, and, in just a few minutes, Carl's visit with the Leuchtags.

You can tell when cognac is being poured in the Café by the bottle—the label reads Napoleon Cognac—as well as the cordial glasses that the house uses instead of snifters. Cognac is brandy that comes from the French Cognac region, so it makes sense that when Renault sees Rick settled in with a bottle he comments that he's pleased to see Rick taking on a Frenchman's ways.

DID YOU KNOW?: After making their way to the bar, Yvonne and her new German escort order a famous World War I-era, champagne-based drink called a French 75. For Yvonne it's a natural, but for a German officer to partake in the enemy's signature drink—why, that's nothing short of treasonous.

The drink takes its name from the 75-millimeter field guns used by the French in the Great War. The French 75 was the best gun in its class, a rare bright spot for the French army in an otherwise dismal five-year military display. In fact, when the Americans finally arrived, they had no comparable field gun and relied heavily on borrowed French 75s. Capable of lobbing dozens of shells per minute, the guns were well-suited for pinning down the advance-minded Germans.

The drink's origin isn't known, though the much-ballyhooed Harry's Bar in Paris (a sometime Hemingway haunt) is not shy to claim credit. What's more, save the champagne, there's not even a consensus on how to make one. Bar guides differ on whether cognac or gin should be used as the drink's secondary ingredient, and some, but not all, call for the use of lemon juice and sugar. We say, since it's named after a French artillery piece, it should be made with cognac. Picture French soldiers along the Western Front sloshing cognac and champagne together in their canteens.

If Sascha goes the traditional route he'll use an ounce or two of cognac, half an ounce of lemon juice and a teaspoon of superfine sugar, all shaken well and poured into an ice-filled Collins glass, then top it with 4-5 ounces of dry champagne.

However you make it, be forewarned: like the field gun it's named after, this drink punishes, the next day included. If Rick thinks Yvonne had too much to drink last night, wait until he sees her after she and her new boyfriend polish off a whole row of French 75s, as she boasts to Sascha.

EXPLANATION REQUIRED: Yvonne sure is excited about her new man, but things turn ugly in a hurry when a French officer at the bar takes offense to her newfound preference for cavorting with the enemy. Speaking in French, Yvonne and the French officer exchange the following terse words:

FRENCH OFFICER. Listen, you are not French, you go with Germans like that!
YVONNE. What are you butting in for?
FRENCH OFFICER. I am butting in for (inaudible)
YVONNE. It's none of your business!

The German officer then confronts the French officer, a fight ensues, and Yvonne exclaims in French, "Stop! I beg of you! I beg of you! Stop!" After Rick breaks up the fight, the French officer gets in a parting shot, yelling in French at the German officer, "Dirty Boche there! We will have our revenge!" Naturally, *boche* is not a compliment—the French had been using this put-down since World War I.

CLOSER LOOK: Turns out that, apart from Yvonne's shameless flaunting of her new boche, er, beau, there's a more immediate reason why the French officer was annoyed with her. As Yvonne explains to Sascha how she wants their drinks served, she inadvertently whacks the French officer's hand with her purse. **(1:02:41)** Until then, the Frenchman seemed more interested in examining the contents of his drink than in picking a fight.

CLOSER LOOK: As the scene unfolds, take time to admire another chic outfit worn by Yvonne. And when she faces the camera just before the fight breaks out, the outfit's main feature—a plunging neckline—is revealed. If her choice of clothes is part of a plan to make Rick jealous, it's not working. He seemed unmoved when she walked past his table a few minutes ago, and he doesn't even look her way as he breaks up the fight.

CLOSER LOOK: Keep an eye on Yvonne just after the slap. You can hear her, but her lips aren't moving. This is the second voice dub for Madeleine LeBeau. Now, the first one may have been due to her heavy French accent—just two years before these scenes were shot she didn't know a stitch of English. But no such excuse here—the dubbed line is actually in French.

JUST WONDERING: If you're a German officer and you've just been insulted in front of your new girl by a guy whose country you just conquered, should your first move in a fight really be a slap to the face? **(1:02:55)** Yvonne could have done that herself.

CLOSER LOOK: Behind the fracas, look for the giant samovar perched on a ledge. **(1:02:51)** Samovars are of Russian origin and used to heat and hold water for tea. They do make them this big, but we're guessing this one is decorative since there's no spigot at the bottom. Note the decorative star and crescent at the top.

There are actually two samovars in the main room, and both are used at various times to cast shadows on the Café's walls. The other one is located just a few feet over from this one, at the bottom of the stairs leading up to Rick's office and apartment. The best view of it is during the scene in which Renault prepares to arrest Ugarte. **(20:44)**

RANDOM THOUGHTS: Not only was smoking an integral part of wartime culture, it also plays a key role in creating an exotic atmosphere in Rick's. Practically everyone at Rick's contributes to the cause. In this scene Renault and Strasser share a smoke as they discuss Victor's future.

So how do the main characters stack up on the tobacco front? Well, we actually went to the trouble of counting the number of smokes partaken by each of them. With these two rules—unlit smokes count, and characters get credit for two smokes when shown smoking throughout an extended scene—here's our tally: Rick—16, Victor—7, Captain Renault—5, Major Strasser—5, Ugarte—3, Ferrari—1.

It's no surprise who the most prolific smoker is—it had to be Rick, if only because he gets the most screen time. Indeed, it's the rare scene in which Rick doesn't have a smoke in his hand. He's even holding one when he shoots Strasser!

As for the also-rans, Victor is Rick's stiffest competition, held back only by his lack of screen time. Renault doesn't get going until the very end of the first night at Rick's, but he makes up for lost time with two at Rick's on the second night and two more in his office on the last day.

Strasser is somewhat of a sneaky smoker, slipping one in here and there, in between threats of bodily harm. Ferrari is the only one who smokes a cigar, perhaps because he does not care to, as he later puts it to Rick, sell cigarettes to himself. And poor Ugarte. Little did he know that the three smokes he enjoyed in the gambling room would be his last ones. Finally, notice who is not on the list. Despite practically swimming in cigarette smoke the entire picture, the refined Ilsa Lund never once takes a puff.

CAST ANECDOTES: The practical reason why Ilsa isn't seen with a cigarette is that, at the time, Bergman was not a smoker. But all that changed a few years later when she experimented with smoking during the filming of *Arch of Triumph* (1948). Now, how she picked up the habit there but managed to avoid it during the *Casablanca* smoke-fest is beyond us. Anyway, once hooked, she was an avid smoker for life.

EXPLANATION REQUIRED: To send the Leuchtags on their way to America, Carl brings them a little going-away present—a cognac on the house. Speaking in German, Carl accompanies the gesture with words that translate to "Here I am again, Mr. Leuchtag. I brought you the finest brandy. Only the employees drink it here." If the Leuchtags stick to their plan of speaking only English from here on out, this may be the last German they hear for a while.

RICK'S CAFÉ—SECOND NIGHT

This second Rick's Café illustration captures Café activity on the second night.

1. Rick's table at beginning of night; also where Renault joins Rick for a drink; also where refugee Annina Brandel seeks advice from Rick.
2. Fight at the bar involving Yvonne.
3. Strasser's table; also where he and his men sing "Die Wacht am Rhein."
4. The Leuchtag's table, with Carl joining.
5. Sam playing "As Time Goes By."
6. Victor and Ilsa's table; also where Strasser confronts Ilsa at end of night.
7. Rick and Victor on stairs outside of Rick's office, watching Strasser and his men sing "Die Wacht am Rhein."
8. Yvonne's table.
9. Victor and the band playing "La Marseillaise."
10. Where Strasser tells Renault to close down the Café.
11. Where Rick and Carl talk after hours about Café operations.

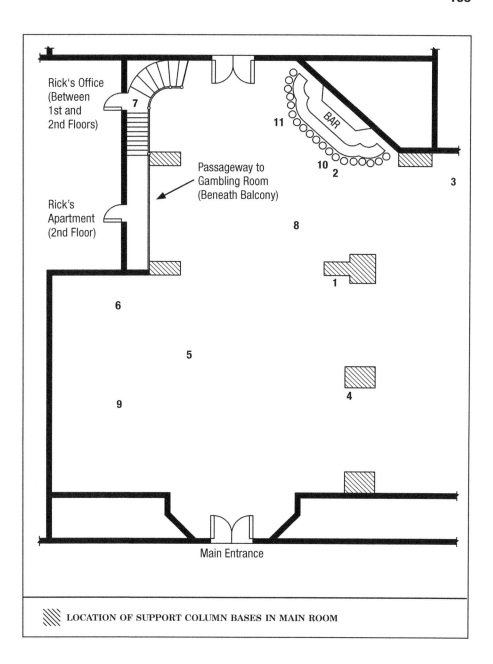

CAST ANECDOTES: Playing the Leuchtags are émigré actors Ludwig Stossel and Ilka Gruning. Both were from Austria-Hungary, with Gruning hailing from Vienna and Stossel from the small Hungarian castle-town of Lockenhaus. After the post-World War I break-up of Austria-Hungary, Lockenhaus and most of the predominantly German-speaking region of Burgenland went to Austria.

Both actors made their way to America in the wake of Germany's 1938 invasion of Austria. Owing to their Jewish heritage, Stossel's extended family in Lockenhaus saw everything they owned seized by the Germans during the Anschluss.

These two actors made for a great screen couple. They have a half dozen or so film credits in common, including *Temptation* (1946), also as husband and wife. In *King's Row* (1942), a Claude Rains feature, Gruning has a nice-sized role and she and Stossel share a few seconds of screen time. Look also for Gruning in *This is the Army* (1943), and for Stossel in *The Pride of the Yankees* (as Lou Gehrig's father) and the Tracy-Hepburn romantic comedy *Woman of the Year*, both released the same year as *Casablanca*.

HISTORY LESSON: Annina is back again in this scene. And this time she seems resigned to secure exit visas from Renault. The way Annina tells it, back in Bulgaria, "the devil has the people by the throat," so who can blame her for being willing to do most anything to avoid going back? Now, with the devil reference she could be referring to Bulgaria's king at the time, Boris III, but our guess is she's talking about Hitler.

Bulgaria and the rest of the Balkan states basically got a pass early in the war on account of Hitler having his hands full with France and Great Britain. But all that changed when, six months after invading Greece, Italy still hadn't finished the job. In April 1941, to shore up his now-exposed southern flank, Hitler invaded Greece himself. And the plan called for German troops stream down from Romania through Bulgaria, one of Greece's northern neighbors. So it makes some sense that Jan and Annina are on the run in December 1941 when *Casablanca* is set.

Just before the invasion, Hitler forced Bulgaria to join the Tripartite Pact. As incentive, Hitler assured Boris III that Bulgaria could retake territory lost to Greece and Yugoslavia in 1913. Less than a month after Hitler invaded those countries, Bulgaria cashed in on the deal. Civilian life in the annexed territories was chaotic and dangerous. And when Germany demanded the deportation of several thousand Jews from the territories to concentration camps, the Bulgarian government capitulated.

As for Bulgaria proper, of all the countries within Hitler's sphere of influence there were far riskier places to be holed up. The Bulgarian government managed to sidestep Germany's demand to deport some tens of thousands of Jews living in Bulgaria. Meanwhile, Bulgaria dragged its feet on supporting Hitler's invasion of Russia, and ultimately avoided front-line duties. In Bulgaria proper, civilian and military deaths were comparatively low. So depending on where in Bulgaria Jan and Annina were coming from, they might have been able to avoid trouble even had they stayed put.

CAST ANECDOTES: Rick gives Annina a hard time for being in the Café under age. In fact, when these scenes were filmed the actress who played Annina, Joy Page, was just seventeen. This was Page's first picture. So how, you ask, does a seventeen-year-old high school senior with no acting experience land a plum role in *Casablanca*? Well, it sure didn't hurt that her stepfather was Jack Warner, the head of Warner Bros. Warner you see, married Page's mother in 1936. Apparently her acting coach recommended that she read for the part, and Warner made it happen.

But it seems there's more to the story. We discovered that since 1939 her birth father, actor Don Alvarado, had been working at Warner Bros. on the production side, mostly as a director's first assistant. Probing further, we discovered to our amazement that Alvarado originally was assigned to *Casablanca* as the director's first assistant for various pre-production screen tests, including those for the role of Annina. And wouldn't you know it, on May 8, 1942, he's listed as the first assistant for his own daughter's screen test. After that, Alvarado mysteriously disappears from the *Casablanca* production sheets.

Meanwhile, Warner made his impact a few days before filming commenced. Wallis and Curtiz still had not decided whether to use Page, so Warner brought the matter to a head by sending the two a telegram with instructions to make a decision that very day. Whether Warner actually wanted them to cast Page in the film is uncertain, but how would you react if the head of the studio forced you to decide the casting fate of his stepdaughter? Not surprisingly, two days later Wallis and Curtiz had Page slated to play Annina.

We will leave critiquing her performance to others, but we will say that the script didn't play to Page's strengths, forcing her to deliver lines that would have been challenging even for seasoned actors. Add in the fact that Page's first big scene was opposite Hollywood giant Humphrey Bogart, and you can see how she might have felt a little out of her comfort zone.

If you want to see Page in one of her seven post-*Casablanca* films, the best of the lot is *The Bullfighter and the Lady* (1950). Tapping into her Mexican heritage, the stunningly beautiful Page shines as the daughter of a bullfighting coach who catches the eye of an American upstart bullfighter.

RANDOM THOUGHTS: Just as Victor and Ilsa arrive at Rick's, Sam starts playing "It Had to Be You." We've heard this signature song a few times by now, but this time the tone is not as upbeat, and in the context of what is transpiring on screen the song takes on a whole new meaning. Of all the people to show up at Rick's, it *had* to be Ilsa.

MUSIC NOTES: "It Had to Be You" is featured in a 1947 film of the same name starring Ginger Rogers. If you love the song and are curious about the film's use of it, you'll be disappointed. Columbia wasted the song on a second-tier farcical romantic comedy that drains the tune of all its power. Rogers mugs her way through the film playing a four-time runaway bride, whose cause seems hopeless until she reconnects (in the most bizarre way) with a childhood crush. Bottom line, stick with *Casablanca* to hear this song in a more pleasing setting.

FILM ANECDOTES: Warner Bros. assigned Hungarian Michael Curtiz to direct this picture largely because he was an expert at creating action and atmosphere, both viewed by producer Hal Wallis as key to the film's success. Curtiz honed these skills early in his career while directing silent films in Austria and Germany.

A native of Budapest, Curtiz made his way to Hollywood by virtue of Jack Warner having viewed one of those films, *Moon of Israel* (1924). Enthralled by Curtiz's unique shooting style, Warner signed him for what turned out to be the beginning of an unprecedented three-decade relationship. Curtiz and Wallis became close friends, though you wouldn't know it from the tone of Wallis' internal communications during the filming of *Casablanca*, where he was not shy about chiding Curtiz for overzealous shooting and unauthorized "do-overs."

Curtiz was Jewish and during the war his family members back in Hungary were not immune from Nazi persecution. Jack Warner is said to have helped Curtiz secure an exit visa for his mother. His sister, brother-in-law and their children were not as fortunate. They were all deported to Auschwitz, though incredibly his sister and one of her children survived.

Famous for his thick Hungarian accent and propensity to butcher the English language (in a scene calling for rider-less horses, he memorably shouted, "Bring on the empty horses!"), Curtiz's best films include the 1928 epic *Noah's Ark, Yankee Doodle Dandy* (released the same year as *Casablanca*), *The Adventures of Robin Hood* (1938, one of eighteen films he directed featuring a swashbuckling Errol Flynn) and *Mildred Pierce* (1945).

Rick's—Gambling Room

EXPLANATION REQUIRED: Back at the roulette table, Emil the croupier is again at the helm. On the first spin he announces in French, "The eight in full. The eight in full. We pay the eight in full." You can see on the table that no one on Jan's side of the wheel has played the eight **(1:08:12)**, and poor Jan has lost again.

Rick then approaches the table to assist Jan with his betting strategy. After some urging, Jan places all his chips on twenty-two. Another spin of the wheel and Emil announces the winners: "Twenty-two, black, even and pass."

Jan lets it all ride. Emil gives the wheel another spin, announces that he's taking no more bets (*Rien ne va plus. Fini.*), and like magic it comes up twenty-two again.

RANDOM THOUGHTS: We are being picky, but the timing is way off on the first spin of the roulette wheel in this scene. When Rick enters the room, Emil calls for a spin of the wheel, and it looks like he's going to do just that. In the next shot he never touches the wheel, yet we hear the ball rattling around for a second or two before Emil and his table hands rake in the bets. Bottom line, there's no allowance for the actual spin, which should take several seconds. It's surely due to tight editing; but whatever the cause, in our strict book it's a gaffe.

CAST ANECDOTES: While Dalio's built-in French accent no doubt gave him the inside track for a role in the film, he had another thing working for him. One of his first roles in Hollywood was the croupier in a film called *The Shanghai Gesture* (1941). His character in that film was Marcel, the Master of the Spinning Wheel. Well, just a year later he parlayed his mastery of the spinning wheel into the role of Emil the croupier in *Casablanca*. Wade through some wince-inducing moments and *The Shanghai Gesture* rewards with dazzling shots of a frenzied casino and Dalio presiding over the featured table. He looks and sounds in this film exactly like Emil in *Casablanca*—he even uses the same table banter. It's just that instead of spinning the wheel at Rick's Café Américain in Casablanca, he's doing it at Mother Gin Sling's Casino in Shanghai.

JUST WONDERING: How exactly does Rick manage to rig the roulette wheel to land on a specific number at will? There are only a few ways to cheat at roulette. One is "past posting," which involves using sleight of hand to make or switch a bet after the outcome has been determined. Another is exploiting a table bias that makes it more probable for certain numbers or colors to hit than others. But neither of these gambits occurs here. Rick knew that the ball would land on twenty-two both times. So short of Emil activating a high-powered magnet, we're stumped on how he and Rick pull this one off.

RANDOM THOUGHTS: So what were the true odds of Jan hitting twenty-two twice in a row? Well, on a European roulette wheel there are thirty-seven possible outcomes on any given roll, zero through thirty-six (American roulette tables also have a double zero). With a desired outcome of hitting twenty-two on consecutive spins, the odds are 1/1,369 (1/37 times 1/37). Good thing Rick had his finger on the wheel.

CAST ANECDOTES: Annina describes Jan earlier as "such a boy," but in fact actor Helmut Dantine was twenty-four to Joy Page's seventeen when these scenes were shot. The dashing Dantine emigrated to America in the late 1930s from his hometown of Vienna when he was around nineteen, effectively a political enemy of the Reich. It seems that Dantine's participation in an anti-Nazi rally or two had him under the Gestapo's watchful eye. Before long he was rounded up and thrown in a local labor camp. He got out of that mess apparently through family connections, but now he was clearly a marked man, and correctly deduced that it would be wise for him to leave Austria.

Given his subdued demeanor and reined-in role, you might think this was his first film. In fact, it was his eighth. What's more, just before *Casablanca* he had a prominent role in another classic, *Mrs. Miniver* (1942), the wartime drama detailing the harrowing days of the Battle of Britain. Dantine plays a downed Luftwaffe pilot who puts a good scare into Mrs. Miniver (Greer Garson) with mad shouts of German superiority and the promise that London will suffer the same fate as the recently rampaged Rotterdam. Seeing his hair-raising performance, it's too bad there wasn't a role in *Casablanca* for a young Luftwaffe assistant to Major Strasser—he and Veidt would have made a fine evil pair.

The fact that *Mrs. Miniver* won Best Picture in 1942 means that Dantine had two Best Picture appearances under his belt just four years into his Hollywood career. Not bad for someone who came to America with zero acting experience.

RANDOM THOUGHTS: Well, this is the last time we see Jan and Annina in the film. Earlier we promised we'd tally their various appearances, and the grand total is...six. In chronological order, they appear: 1) in the black market, just before the suspect is gunned down; 2) outside the prefect's office watching Strasser's plane; 3) inside the prefect's office seeking exit visas; 4) in the Blue Parrot seeking exit visas from Ferrari; 5) in the main room of the Café (Annina only) talking with Rick; and 6) here, in the gambling room.

If their cinematic journey seems a little disjointed, here's why. As mentioned earlier, in the original play the couple was very much involved in goings on. And early scripts for the film followed that lead and had the couple slated for more screen time. But over time their scenes were pared down, which caused the storyline to lose cohesion and made it seem like the couple was randomly ducking in and out of the action.

Rick's—Main Room

MUSIC NOTES: As we return to the main room, listen for the aforementioned reprise (from last night) of the song "The Very Thought of You."

CAST ANECDOTES: Sascha is so pleased with what Rick has done for Jan and Annina that he gives his boss a kiss. Rick shrugs it off, calling him a "crazy Russian." Lioned Kinskey, who plays Sascha, must have felt right at home being on the receiving end of this line because he was from St. Petersburg, Russia, and his nickname was the Mad Russian.

Kinskey too left his homeland on account of war, but it wasn't World War II. Instead, his emigration to America had ties to World War I and the 1917 Bolshevik Revolution. Coming off Russia's miserable four-year slog through World War I, St. Petersburg was not such a fun place to live. When the Bolsheviks seized control of the city and government in October 1917 with the political agenda of getting Russia out of the war, you might think this would be progress.

Unfortunately, the revolution sparked a *civil* war that lasted through 1920. And this was not your average civil war, accounting for as many as nine million deaths from war, famine and disease. Kinskey was not alone in his decision to leave. Between one and two million Russians—mostly from the upper and middle class—fled Russia for safer environs during this time.

To see Kinskey playing a revolutionary, check out the Marx Brothers' *Duck Soup* (1933), where he is tasked with taking down Freedonia. Find him as well in *Algiers* (1938) and two 1941 films he shares with S.Z. Sakall, *That Night in Rio* and *Ball of Fire*.

CLOSER LOOK: Look for the bottles resting on the bar labeled Bitters, Lime and Absinthe. **(1:10:08)** Absinthe?! Now that's no ordinary drink. Absinthe is a highly potent liquor, usually upwards of 150 proof. For that reason alone it's sure to knock even a professional drinker like Ugarte on his tail. Emerald green in color, absinthe has a licorice taste and usually is downed on the rocks with a healthy dose of sugar to offset its bitterness.

In the mid-1800s this drink was all the rage in Europe, particularly in Paris where "happy hour" became known as "the green hour." But as it gained popularity, absinthe developed a reputation for being a highly-addictive hallucinogenic with a tendency to make regular consumers, well, crazy. Van Gogh is said to have been drinking absinthe when he decided one ear was plenty.

Then in 1905, a man in Switzerland murdered his wife and children. Absinthe was blamed. Everyone panicked and before long the so-called Absinthe Murders touched off a movement to ban the stuff. And within a few years absinthe was banned in America and most of Europe, including France. (No small trick given that it was basically France's national drink.) These days the prevailing theory is that things were slightly exaggerated and the crazy behavior was largely just drunks being drunks.

Now, whether absinthe should have been available in Rick's in 1941 is an open question. It was banned in France at the time, and presumably that ban would cover French protectorates. Whatever the case, keep an eye out for signs of *absinthism* amongst Rick's regulars.

MUSIC NOTES: The second fight of the night in the Café is a battle of patriotic songs. The German officers delight in "Die Wacht am Rhein," while those sympathetic to France counter with "La Marseillaise." Both are soaked with the jingoistic declarations you'd expect from such songs. But how their patriotic messages are conveyed is quite different.

Written in 1840, "Die Wacht am Rhein" is about Germany's fear at the time that the French were going to seize the ever-coveted left bank of the Rhine. Basically, the song says, "Hey, let's not let the French take our river!" It was the unofficial anthem of the Second Reich, and served as the rally cry for German troops during World War I. Here's the translation of the lyrics that can be heard in the film:

> *The cry roars like thunder*
> *Like ringing swords and crashing waves*
> *To the Rhine! To the Rhine,*
> *To the German Rhine!*
> *Who will be the river's guardian?*
> *Dear Fatherland be calm*
> *Dear Fatherland be calm*
> *Firmly and faithfully stands the watch,*
> *The watch on the Rhine*
> *Firm and true stands the watch,*
> *The watch on the Rhine!*

"La Marseillaise" is a revolutionary battle song dating back to the days of the French Revolution. It became France's national song in 1795, but its revolutionary roots caused it to be banned a few times during the Napoleonic era. In 1879, the Third Republic saw fit to reinstall it as the national anthem, and that was that. One of the finest national anthems ever penned. But, oh, the lyrics! If you're inclined to think that the Germans would write the more aggressive anthem, check out this creepy stuff:

> *Let us go, children of the Fatherland*
> *The day of glory has arrived*
> *Of the tyranny now against us*
> *The blood-stained flag has been raised*
> *The blood-stained flag has been raised*
> *Do you hear in the countryside*
> *Those raging cut-throat soldiers coming?*
> *To slaughter your children.*
> *And your companions!*
> *To arms, citizens!*
> *Form the battalions!*
> *March on, march on!*
> *That their impure blood*
> *Should water your furrows!*

Wow! If the French fought like they wrote, they wouldn't have had a problem in either world war. And make no mistake, it was penned with the Germans in mind. So it's no wonder Strasser's next move after hearing this choral assault was to shut down the Café.

MUSIC NOTES: If the cinematic goal here was to have a showdown between French and German national anthems, "Die Wacht am Rhein" was not the correct choice. The song was never Germany's official national anthem, and in fact was disfavored by the Third Reich due to its association with the Second Reich.

Instead, the appropriate counter balance would have been one of two songs, "Das Lied der Deutschen" or "Horst Wessel Lied." In 1922, "Das Lied der Deutschen" (better known as "Deutschland Uber Alles") became Germany's official national anthem. In 1931, the Nazis made "Horst Wessel Lied" the party's official anthem, before elevating it to co-national anthem status in 1933. The production team was aware of all this but was concerned about potential copyright issues with the anthems.

Still, music director Max Steiner did manage to weave in a melodic quotation from "Das Lied der Deutschen" as one of the menacing German themes. You can hear a quotation here as Strasser tracks down Renault and orders him to close the Café. **(1:13:55)** Listen for it in these scenes as well: the Paris flashback, in the Café the first night as Rick and Ilsa discuss the day the Germans marched into Paris and one last time at the airport, just after Rick and Strasser's duel.

Finally, we have to give Steiner credit for going with extra mile with this scene. Not satisfied with having the songs simply play over each other, he actually went to the trouble of synchronizing the songs for a brief moment, thus avoiding a cacophonic mess, before "La Marseillaise" takes charge.

JUST WONDERING: Might Sam be a little upset to see the German officers commandeer his piano and use it to bang out a German war anthem? **(1:12:18)** The piano has been on the other side of the room for most of the film, but the Germans must have seized it when Sam was on a break.

CLOSER LOOK: Turns out the house band is far more talented than we thought. This is a six-piece band—piano, trombone, trumpet, clarinet, accordion and drums (seven if you count the guitarist). But by the end of "La Marseillaise," they have magically transformed into what sounds like a full orchestra, crashing cymbals and all. Now that's talent.

MUSIC NOTES: A similar showdown between these two songs occurs in *Grand Illusion* (1937), the World War I classic we mentioned earlier that features Marcel Dalio. In that film, French POWs learn of a military setback on the front, and overhear their gloating German captors singing "Die Wacht am Rhein." A day or so later at a POW-produced stage show, the POWs learn that French troops have turned the tide. The heartening news prompts the POWs to break into a rousing rendition of "La Marseillaise," to the considerable dismay of the German officers in attendance. Though the songs are not sung at the same time, the stirrings of hope and empowerment are the same.

CLOSER LOOK: During the dueling performances we spied another film gaffe. In a long shot of the men singing, an older couple sits at the first table on the right side. But just a few seconds later we find a now-remorseful Yvonne and her new German beau at the same table. The two have moved on from French 75s to a bottle of champagne. And while Yvonne can't bear to watch the display, the German officer is, of course, having a fine time. Watch for him toasting his fellow officers.

JUST WONDERING: Is Yvonne hot and cold on French patriotism, or what? Here she's positively a mess as she sings "La Marseillaise." But just moments earlier she was shamelessly hanging on the arm of a German officer. Come on, Yvonne, pick a side here.

CAST ANECDOTES: Actually, quite understandably this scene was an emotional undertaking for France native Madeleine LeBeau. According to Marcel Dalio, LeBeau cried with each singing of "La Marseillaise."

EXPLANATION REQUIRED: After the songs are over Strasser tracks down Ilsa, warning her that the only safe way for Victor to leave Casablanca is to travel back to occupied France "under safe conduct from me." "Safe conduct" papers were travel papers issued by German and French military authorities. Foreigners had to possess them in order to move about legally within France. French authorities could demand the papers at any time, and if you couldn't produce them you were likely to end up in a concentration camp. Of course, Strasser's notion of safe conduct for Victor adds up to a trip to a concentration camp regardless.

DID YOU KNOW?: Strasser also says that if Victor does not agree to return with him to occupied France, alternatively Victor could find himself in a local concentration camp. This statement is accurate. The Germans and the Vichy government together accounted for dozens of internment camps strewn across Algeria, Tunisia and Morocco, including a few in the Casablanca area. Most were forced labor camps, some of which were used to support rail line construction in the Morocco-Algeria border region. So on Strasser's whim, Victor could be laying rail ties in the desert for the Vichy government's failed attempt to build a Trans-Sahara railway.

RANDOM THOUGHTS: Ilsa's choice of outfits in this scene, a paisley blouse paired with a bullfighter's sash, is certainly a bold choice. The women's gowns in the film were designed by an Australian costume designer with an unusual and hyphenated name, Orry-Kelly. He was the head designer at Warner Bros. in the 30s and 40s, outfitting the studio's leading ladies. Aside from designing fabulous gowns, Orry-Kelly's other claim to fame was being Cary Grant's long-time roommate (and reportedly more) when Grant was still known as Archie Leach.

FILM ANECDOTES: Going into production the script included a brief gag scene after Ilsa and Victor leave. As everyone files out of the Café the German officer who was with Yvonne earlier orders one last drink from Sascha. The officer insists on being served the concoction that Sascha is mischievously mixing (absinthe perhaps?), downs it without hesitation, and immediately goes into convulsions before making a mad dash for the door. Ah, Sascha. Apparently, this is payback for socializing with Yvonne.

However, producer Hal Wallis wasn't buying this gag at all, complaining that he didn't think they could get anything out of the "Mickey Finn" business. Once again Wallis' wishes prevailed, and the bit was dropped. If you want to see the deleted scene, you actually can. This is one of just a few film outtakes that survived, and can be found (though without sound) in the bonus materials for special edition *Casablanca* offerings.

Victor and Ilsa's Hotel Room

RANDOM THOUGHTS: As the film spirals toward the climatic scene, it's still anybody's guess how this Rick-Ilsa-Victor love triangle is going to shake out. We know where Victor stands, but Rick and Ilsa remain tough reads. If this scene is any indication of which way Ilsa is leaning, it's not looking so good for Victor.

It's not what Ilsa says; it's what she *doesn't* say. First, with emotions running high Victor tells Ilsa how much he loves her. But Ilsa does not have it in her to respond in kind, and instead meekly offers that, yes, she knows he loves her. Ouch! That's the kind of hollow, missing-the-point response one hears right before one gets dumped. And it's actually the second time today she has done this. At the Blue Parrot, Victor's declaration of love elicited from Ilsa this cheeky response: "Your secret will be safe with me."

Then Ilsa subjects Victor to more emotional torment. Just as Victor heads out the door, she shouts for him and rushes to stop him, as if she has something she simply must tell him...perhaps that she really *does* love him. Um, no. "Be careful," she says, which is only slightly more heartfelt than "Don't forget your hat." It's just not in Ilsa's heart right now to tell her husband she loves him.

JUST WONDERING: If Victor wants to avoid being followed, wouldn't he be wise to slip out of the hotel a different way? He just spied a German operative lurking below his hotel room. Yet on his way to the secret Resistance meeting Victor elects to walk past the very spot where the man stood.

Rick's—Main Room

CLOSER LOOK: The initial shot of Rick and Carl going over the books near the bar is a unique perspective. It's taken through the glass panes of the main room's rear doorway; Rick actually secures the doors at the very start of the scene. While the doorway is visible in numerous scenes, only one person actually uses it—a gendarme who exits the main room through it in preparation for Ugarte's arrest. Well, we know that the doorway beneath the balcony leads to the gambling room, but, unfortunately, we never learn what rooms are accessible through this rear doorway.

JUST WONDERING: So how are we able to hear Rick and Carl's initial exchange so well given that we are on the other side of the doors?

CLOSER LOOK: We have actually seen this filming technique before. The first scene set in Renault's office opens with a shot of Strasser and Renault that's taken from outside the office, through a wood-barred window or opening. **(51:03)** Seconds later, the next shot transports us inside the office.

Similarly, in the Café on the first night, when Rick and Renault head up the stairs to Rick's office, the camera shoots through an opening in the wall where the stairs turn. The camera then pulls back to the other side of the wall and into Rick's office, and, like magic, we see them enter. How cool is that?! Both on the stairs and in the office, it's like we're crouched in the corner.

We love this technique as it adds to the sense that we moviegoers are right there, sneaking around Casablanca, spying on the action.

RANDOM THOUGHTS: We have sensed along the way that Carl is a star employee, and here we learn that Rick trusts Carl enough to have him handle the Café's bookkeeping. And it's a good thing he's so trustworthy because later tonight Rick will be relying on Carl to help him out of quite a jam—Ilsa in Rick's apartment, with Victor downstairs at the bar—and Rick will definitely need Carl to keep that under wraps.

Rick's—Rick's Apartment

CLOSER LOOK: So how does Ilsa manage to get her hands on a gun? The answer can be found during the scene that just took place in Victor and Ilsa's hotel room. Victor leaves for the secret meeting; Ilsa grabs her coat and fetches her purse from a table. She then opens the table's drawer, grabs a gun, and stuffs it into her purse. **(1:18:40)** Look for the purse in her left hand at the beginning of this scene. **(1:15:36)** So Victor apparently has managed to hang on to this weapon despite being under the Gestapo's full scrutiny.

JUST WONDERING: Is there more between Rick and Ilsa in this scene than a kiss? We'll never know for sure, but when the film cuts directly from the couple locking lips to Rick enjoying a smoke at the window with the airport beacon suddenly in full swing, it's hard not to conclude that this is 1940s Hollywood code for, "these two just hooked up." Looking for further support? Check out the champagne bottle and glasses on the table.

Of course, Hollywood was not above using cigarettes and drinks as surrogates for sex. For a tutorial on this, see Bette Davis and Paul Henreid puffing away together in *Now, Voyager*. But Ilsa is a married woman. Indeed, production records show that the film censorship wonks wanted to eliminate any suggestion in this scene of a sexual affair between Rick and Ilsa. Somehow Warner Bros. managed to keep this scene intact.

CAST ANECDOTES: Though she never took on refugee status, Ingrid Bergman did have a harrowing European wartime travel tale. In August 1939, after making her first Hollywood film, *Intermezzo*, Bergman returned to Sweden to reunite with her husband and daughter. But just one month after her return Germany overran Poland, and World War II was on. Two months later Russia invaded Sweden's neighbor, Finland, and suddenly Sweden wasn't looking like the greatest place to hang out as the world powers settled their differences.

In late December 1939, with Sweden quickly becoming convenient to nowhere, Bergman again left her homeland for America. Traveling through Germany and its recent conquest, Austria, she made her way to Genoa, Italy. There, on January 2, 1940, she caught the Italian liner *SS Rex*, which happened to make an unscheduled stop in Lisbon of all places before sailing for New York. Her decision to leave Sweden proved to be a fortuitous one for her and us. Had she stuck around much longer she would have been trapped by the war, and would never have made it to America to take on the role of Ilsa.

FILM ANECDOTES: Time to examine how casting transpired for the role of Rick Blaine. Thanks to Warner Bros. producer Hal Wallis, it was never seriously in doubt that Bogart would get the role. Bogart had been under contract with Warner Bros. for years, and Wallis was convinced that Bogart's tough-guy persona was just right for Rick. Film lore has it that Ronald Reagan was the original choice. While it's true that Warner Bros. floated Reagan's name in an early press release, he was never seriously considered.

If anyone had a shot at the part it was George Raft, Bogart's some-time rival at Warner Bros. Raft had a reputation for rejecting roles, often to his detriment. Raft had first crack at playing Sam Spade in *The Maltese Falcon*, but concluded that the film wasn't sufficiently weighty. That left the door open for Bogart, who landed the part and turned it into a career-making role.

But in a rare good call, Raft lobbied studio head Jack Warner to play Rick Blaine. When Warner floated the idea to Wallis, Wallis dashed off an emphatic memo to Warner, urging, "Bogart is ideal for [*Casablanca*] and it is being written for him, and I think we should forget Raft for this property." And that was the end of the matter.

RANDOM THOUGHTS: So could Raft have pulled off playing Rick? Not a chance. To see why, check out *Outpost in Morocco* (1949), which features Raft gallivanting through the Moroccan desert as a Foreign Legion officer assigned to ensure the safety of a desert princess. One scene has a waning and overstuffed Raft sauntering around a café reminiscent of Rick's, sporting a white tuxedo, à la Rick, and dropping bad pick-up lines and hand-kisses on the princess. Yvonne may have bought his shtick, but Ilsa? Never.

FILM ANECDOTES: Casting for the role of Ilsa did take a few turns. Warner Bros. originally envisioned Ilsa as American, and had the uninspired idea of plugging in one of its own leading ladies, Ann Sheridan. The studio then got keen on Ilsa being European, and considered Austro-Hungarian Hedy Lamarr and French beauties Michèle Morgan and Edwige Feuillère. Less than two months before filming started, *Casablanca* screenwriters Julius and Phillip Epstein weighed in with Bergman, perhaps looking to ensure the role was cast in their eye. The Epstein brothers urged Hollywood producer David Selznick to loan out Bergman, and two weeks later Warner Bros. and Selznick agreed to an "even swap" of talents—Bergman for Warner Bros. starlet Olivia de Havilland, essentially for one picture.

RANDOM THOUGHTS: So how did the "even swap" of Bergman for de Havilland turn out? Well, we know Warner Bros. got from Bergman a performance for the ages. But what about Selznick? Just a few years earlier Warner Bros. loaned de Havilland to Selznick, and de Havilland delivered an Academy Award-nominated performance in *Gone With the Wind*. But this time Selznick sold his rights to de Havilland to RKO Studios, which in turn assigned de Havilland to a wartime comedy clunker called *Government Girl* (1944). It did okay at the box office, but it ain't no *Casablanca*.

De Havilland, who had a long history of balking at roles she perceived as being below her talents, accused Selznick of scheming to stick her with the middling *Government Girl* assignment while profiting mightily from it. In a scathing letter to de Havilland's agent, Selznick insisted he'd done nothing of the sort, pointing out that he'd have been much better off foregoing the swap and just charging market price for Bergman. Makes sense, but Jack Warner definitely was not known for paying market price.

CAST ANECDOTES: While Ilsa and Rick make up for lost time, let's examine the romantic lives of Bergman and Bogart. Bergman married three times, though it seemed like far more owing to her having accommodated a few trysts along the way. In 1936, at the age of twenty she married fellow Swede Petter Lindstrom, a smart, dashing bachelor several years her senior. Lindstrom played an active role in her transition to American film. But once Bergman got to Hollywood, Lindstrom started looking rather pale in comparison to the men now encircling Bergman. Indeed, Lindstrom basically found himself playing Victor Laszlo to a field of Ricks. Not even a career in neurosurgery could compete with the likes of actor Gary Cooper, director Victor Fleming, and daring D-Day photographer Robert Capa.

In 1949, the seemingly inevitable happened. Bergman screened a film by director Roberto Rossellini and developed an instant crush. After some shameless courting right under Lindstrom's nose, Bergman and Rossellini inked a film deal, which kicked off that spring in Italy with *Stromboli*. Of course, this was merely a pretext for these two to convene without pesky interruptions by Bergman's husband. And before you knew it Bergman was pregnant with Rossellini's child (actually two), and penning a letter to Lindstrom in the same vein as Ilsa's note to Rick.

A prudish American public was incensed by her transgressions, and when U.S. senators began citing "moral turpitude" provisions of U.S. immigration laws as possible grounds for arresting Bergman upon her return to America, she took the hint and steered clear of America for some eight years.

Bergman's films under Rossellini's directorship were not of top caliber, and at home Rossellini proved to be a volatile husband who was more controlling than the one she left. For a time she made it work by taking a page out of Ilsa's book and having Rossellini make the hard decisions for both of them. A Rossellini affair led to their calling it quits in 1958, but not without a bitter child custody dispute. Her third marriage, in 1958 to Swedish theater producer Lars Schmidt, must have felt like paradise after the high drama of the first two.

CAST ANECDOTES: For Bogart the marriage trail was equally well traveled. Of his four marriages, the first two were to talented flapper-type actresses from his New York theater days. Both marriages were doomed largely by divergent career paths. Not having been subjected to any dramatic Paris-train-station style dumpings, Bogart managed to salvage friendships with both women.

His third wife, second-tier Hollywood actress Mayo Methot, was a short-tempered drinker who caused Bogart trouble from the outset. But whereas Rick Blaine would have sent her packing in a heartbeat (think Yvonne), Bogart never could pull the trigger. So in 1938 he married her, seemingly with the hope that it would put a stop to the haranguing. It did not.

The marriage was doomed from the beginning, and it was just a matter of time before Bogart tapped into some of that Rick Blaine Paris flashback charm. And so he did in 1944, when at the age of forty-five he was cast opposite upstart nineteen-year old starlet Lauren Bacall in *To Have and Have Not*. From day one the still-married Bogart was smitten, and a discreet if not totally clandestine romance ensued.

CAST ANECDOTES: *Casablanca* actor Marcel Dalio was also in the cast of *To Have and Have Not*, and recalled Bacall inviting him out for drinks several times during shooting, invitations he happily accepted. But inevitably Bogart would show up, and it didn't take long for Dalio to realize that he was not the one being eyed by Bacall. Dalio resigned himself to playing the role of the "candlestick," thus allowing the couple some quality time together without fear of landing in the gossip columns. With help from Dalio and others, Bogart and Bacall made their May-December romance permanent just one year later.

RANDOM THOUGHTS: Ilsa does not wear a ring while in Paris, which is plausible given that she thought Victor was dead. She does wear one during her stay in *Casablanca*. But while you would expect it to be on her ring finger now that she's reunited with her husband, it's actually on the little finger of her right hand. (It's hard to see in this scene but it's visible in most others.) Now, Norwegians do wear wedding rings on their right hand, but on the ring finger not the little one.

Rick's—Main Room

CLOSER LOOK: The Casablanca police car that speeds by a hiding Carl and Victor is the same one we saw in the market at the beginning of the film during the suspect round-up. This is confirmed by the town car's license plate—7715.M4—which is visible in both scenes. **(2:56; 1:25:40)**

JUST WONDERING: If you were being chased by swarm of German-backed gendarmes, is there anyone who would make for a worse wingman than the oversized and anything-but-nimble Carl?

CLOSER LOOK: Victor does manage to slip the authorities here, but not without injury. You can tell outside that he's hurt his right hand, and in a moment he'll explain that he cut it crawling through a window when gendarmes broke up the Resistance meeting at the *caverne du bois*.

But it looks like his hand is not the only casualty. Check out the right side of Victor's favorite suit coat—two small but prominent bloodstains (confirmed through stills from this scene) caused by his cut hand. **(1:25:43)** Moments later, though, as Victor tends to his wound, the stains have miraculously disappeared.

CLOSER LOOK: The location of the driveway from which Victor and Carl enter the Café raises continuity issues. The script indicates that the two are entering the Café through the back door. In fact, they appear to be coming through a side door. The problem is that this side door entrance has them entering the main room from what was earlier portrayed as the entrance to the gambling room.

CAST ANECDOTES: Playing Carl the waiter is Budapest, Hungary native S.Z. Sakall. With his famous wriggling jowls and ample belly, it's hard to believe that "Cuddles" (a nickname given to him by Jack Warner) actually engaged in trench warfare on the Eastern Front during World War I, helping the Austro-Hungarian army push back the Russians. Of his many wartime stories, our favorite is the visual of a petrified Sakall weaving his way across no-man's land waving a handkerchief with a five-pound keg of vodka slung around his neck, a gift for his Russian adversaries. The perfect man for the job, as no one on the Russian side could have believed by the sight of him that he meant any harm.

Sakall was tapped for *Casablanca* after filming began. The production team thought the film needed some additional comedic relief, and few were better than Sakall at consistently evoking laughs. As a European immigrant he was of course a great fit for the film, but he had a few other things going for him as well. For one, he was fresh off of providing Warner Bros. with some nice comedic scenes in the popular James Cagney musical *Yankee Doodle Dandy* (1942). For another, it didn't hurt that *Casablanca* director Michael Curtiz (who also directed *Yankee Doodle Dandy*) was Sakall's childhood friend from Budapest.

He began his comedic acting career in the theater, first in Budapest and then in Vienna, before parlaying his newly-learned German into theater gigs in Berlin. He caught the film bug in 1922 when he stumbled across his compatriot Curtiz directing on-location in Vienna for the silent film *Sodom and Gomorrah*.

During the 1930s Sakall wrote and acted for Germany's largest film studio, and eventually owned a theater and a film company. As the story goes, after one of his films bombed at its German premiere, Sakall was chased down by Hitler outside the theater. Hitler yelled, "S-S-Sakall!... S-S-Sakall! Aren't you ashamed to make such a stupid senseless picture?!" Sakall tried to laugh it off, kidding with his wife that surely Hitler wouldn't shoot him just for making a bad film. But she was not so sure, thinking that with Hitler nothing was out of the question. Shortly thereafter the two headed back to Vienna. When he saw the same things in Vienna that he had witnessed in Berlin—Nazi flags, Hitler's "brownshirts," constant flare-ups in the streets—he knew that it was time to leave there, too.

He made one picture in England before Universal Pictures asked him to come to America for a film called *It's a Date* (1940). On May 13, 1939, Sakall and his wife left Rotterdam for New York aboard the *Nieuwe Amsterdam*. But the war soon loomed over their Hollywood adventure. During the war they had no contact with their loved ones back in Hungary. Shortly after the war ended came terrible news. His sister's daughter, his wife's brother and sister, her daughter and untold friends were all gone, victims of war murders.

You can pick nearly any film featuring Sakall and he's bound to make you laugh. To sample his comedic skills, check out *Yankee Doodle Dandy*, *Christmas in Connecticut* (1945, with Sidney Greenstreet), *In the Good Old Summertime* (1949), and a few lesser-known ones like *The Devil and Miss Jones* (1941) and *Never Say Goodbye* (1946).

CAST ANEDCOTES: The war may have ruled out any on-location filming in Casablanca, but Bogart did manage to visit the Moroccan city in 1943. Eager to contribute to the war effort, Bogart pressed the studio for leave to entertain the troops overseas. The result was a ten-week tour of North Africa and Italy, spanning the 1943 holiday season and all of January 1944. Casablanca, Dakar and Algiers were among the North Africa stops. Bogart liked to point out that he visited the city before he ever viewed the film, which he finally did shortly after his return home.

CAST ANECDOTES: Bogart's tour was not your typical USO production. No Bob Hope or Andrew Sisters. Just Bogart, his wife Mayo, who came with stage skills, and two USO regulars—a champion trick roper named Don Cummings and an accordionist.

Bogart went to great lengths to boost spirits, including hosting late-night gatherings, which must have been epic. Troop morale in North Africa was decent, with their hard-fought victory behind them. But in Italy the war was raging, the mood was grim and the battle-fatigued soldiers sometimes made for tough audiences.

Check out these war diary excerpts from an Air Force bombardment group, then based in Vincenzo, Italy, which confirm both that the troupe was a hit and that by the end of January it was time to go home:

> Humphrey Bogart and his wife, Mayo Methot appeared in person down at Group headquarters in the afternoon. The men enjoyed the show very much...Hollywood stars are beginning to make their presence known in this area and we were privileged to have...Humphrey Bogart and company [on January 29]....Humphrey Bogart, his wife (Mayo Methot) and Don Cummings suffered from colds and trouper-fatigue but their efforts were appreciated nonetheless. For a screw-ball comedian, red-headed Don Cummings tops the list of any we've seen.

Well, there you have it—on that day anyway, the trick roper really stole the show.

RANDOM THOUGHTS: So do you think during the tour the Bogarts were able to set aside their combative ways? Nah. Accounts had the couple behaving true to their Battling Bogarts nickname. One airman who hopped a plane with them in Italy summed up the encounter this way: "They argued back and forth until I finally got tired of it."

CAST ANECDOTES: Bogart's somewhat brash nature apparently didn't go over too well at times with Army brass. One incident, among several, had an over-served Bogart giving an officer some serious guff after being ordered to shut down a late-night hotel party. The run-ins eventually led to the tour wrapping up earlier than planned.

CHAPTER 7

THE PLANE TO LISBON

> "Last night we said a great many things.
> You said I was to do the thinking for both of us.
> Well, I've done a lot of it since then, and it all adds up to one thing."
> — Rick (to Ilsa)

Rick has now seen and heard everything he needs to know to solve the dilemma of two letters of transit for three people. He's been put through the wringer these last few days, but the future is clear. Rick has a plan but unfortunately he's keeping it close to the vest right now, so we'll have to tag along and see how things unfold.

Rick sets things in motion with a visit to Captain Renault's office, where he makes the following pitch to Renault. Rick has the letters of transit and intends to use them for himself and Ilsa. But Ilsa's ties to Victor present a risk that the Germans will detain them. So if Renault will aid their passage, Rick will enable Renault to arrest Victor on more serious charges. Here, Rick proposes that Renault let Victor out of jail. Rick will then arrange a meeting with Victor to sell him the letters of transit. Renault will swoop in and arrest Victor, instantly earning Major Strasser's favor. Renault is skeptical, but ultimately he bites.

With Renault on board, Rick heads to the Blue Parrot to finalize what is, by Casablanca standards, a blockbuster deal. Rick is selling the Café to Ferrari. Hmmm. Rick must be serious about leaving town.

Finally, Rick makes his way to the Café where, as planned, the freshly sprung Victor meets him. Rick tells Victor he can have the transit papers. But before the transaction is complete, Renault comes out of hiding and arrests Victor. All signs point to Victor heading back to the pen, the victim of a classic setup. As Renault beams over his accomplishment Rick pulls a gun on him, revealing his plan's double-crossing twist.

So far everything is tracking nicely for Rick. Ah, but there's no such thing as a perfect crime, and Rick missteps by allowing Renault to call for a car to the airport. Renault fakes the call, and rings Strasser instead. From the details Strasser knows that something is afoot at the airport involving the letters of transit, and heads that way.

Meanwhile, Rick orders everyone to the airport, where the plane scheduled for Lisbon will be taking off in ten minutes. Who will be on that plane? Rick and Ilsa? Victor and Ilsa? Rick and Victor?! Well, at last we get our answer. Rick tells Ilsa that she will be better off staying with Victor. Ilsa is stunned. Apparently she did some thinking of her own, and came to a different conclusion.

After some smooth talking by Rick, the matter is settled. Rick is staying; Victor and Ilsa are going. But before they can board, Strasser arrives and tries to call the radio tower to stop the plane. Rick orders him off the phone, and backs up the demand with a pistol. When Strasser brandishes a gun of his own, Rick silences the major.

With one problem solved, another is created. How will Renault react to Rick offing Strasser? The answer comes when the gendarmes arrive. Renault gives his familiar order to "round up the usual suspects," and instantly we know that Renault has just stuck his neck out for Rick.

All that is left now is for Renault and Rick to see the plane off. As Victor and Ilsa disappear into the Casablanca fog, Renault and Rick leave the airport together. Renault and Rick both realize that their futures have changed dramatically in the last hour. Renault is now firmly in the Free France camp, while Rick is headed home loveless. Recognizing that there will be lots of questions to answer surrounding Strasser's death, Renault floats the prospect of the two skipping town. And with that, we have witnessed the beginning of a beautiful friendship.

Captain Renault's Office

FILM ANECDOTES: After Rick seemingly secures Captain Renault's buy-in to his plan, he tells Renault that he's heading straight over to the prison to meet with Victor. Remember, Victor was arrested in the Café just last night. In the original script, the next scene picked up on Rick's parting comment and showed him visiting Victor in the pen. The jailhouse scene was filmed, but eventually got dropped.

From the script, here's how the deleted scene unfolds. Rick explains to a now-incarcerated Victor that he's secured his release with a bribe and will sell him the letters of transit for 100,000 francs. He then instructs Victor to meet him at the Café a few minutes before the plane scheduled for Lisbon takes off. Victor worries that he will be shadowed, but Rick assures him that he's taken care of that. Meanwhile, Renault monitors their conversation from his office, and is quite pleased to hear the plan unfolding just as Rick had promised. Warner Bros. filmed the scene before opting to cut it, and an outtake can be found on special edition *Casablanca* offerings, though without sound or the snippet of Renault eavesdropping.

The Blue Parrot

DID YOU KNOW?: Another visit to the Blue Parrot means another gratuitous parrot shot. But this is not the same parrot that kicked off our first visit. The first one was a macaw; this one is an Amazon parrot. And of the many species of Amazon parrots, our bet is on it being a yellow-naped parrot. Disappointingly, these parrots have no blue plumage; they are all green saving, of course, the nape.

CLOSER LOOK: There's quite a bit of signage on the wall outside Ferrari's office, mostly in French and maddeningly illegible. But once again we've done the heavy lifting for you. Here are the translations for what we managed to decipher:

- Drink Cold Zobi
- Ask a Parrot—The Liquor Brand of Morocco
- Coffee of Brazil—Love of the Finest
- Taste our Wines of Algeria—Glass 1 franc

Enjoy a few of the above at the Blue Parrot by day, and you'll be primed for Champagne Cocktails at Rick's by night.

CLOSER LOOK: Earlier we noted the ceramic parrot on Ferrari's desk. Look for it here as Rick and Ferrari finalize their deal.

RANDOM THOUGHTS: Selling the Café to Ferrari is an interesting twist. It must mean that Rick has decided to leave town regardless, either as a fresh start or because he thinks he's in so deep that he'll have no choice. That being the case, Rick might as well have used the sale as part of the ruse by mentioning it to Renault in his office as a way to convince Renault that he really is leaving with Ilsa. In any event, let's hope Rick is certain about this blockbuster deal—if he gets seller's remorse, talking Ferrari out of this goldmine of a Café is not going to be easy.

Rick's—Main Room

RANDOM THOUGHTS: What if Ilsa had stuck to her guns and refused to get on the plane? How would things have unfolded at the airport? Let's survey the options: i) Victor leaves by himself; ii) Rick leaves by himself; iii) Rick and Victor leave together; iv) everybody stays. Victor is an honorable man, and he would never leave his wife behind, especially under such dangerous conditions. The second option just doesn't seem like something our Ricky would do. The third is an amusing prospect but solves nothing—Ilsa is still in harm's way, and no one gets the girl. Besides, leaving Ilsa in Renault's care definitely is not recommended. So we're guessing that, had she stayed, everyone would have headed back to the Café for champagne, cognac and Cointreau.

CLOSER LOOK: We are almost at the end of the film and finally we get a glimpse of the thing that has caused all the commotion in this film, the letters of transit. At a table Rick reviews the letters to make sure everything is in order. Visible on the letter Rick eyes is *Etat Français*, another name for the Vichy government. **(1:32:18)** The envelope for the letters is stamped, quite understandably, with the French words *Confidentiel* and *Secret*.

Major Strasser's Office

CLOSER LOOK: Earlier we revealed that Herr Heinz has ties to the armistice commission, and here's how we knew that. When Renault tries to torpedo Rick's plan by calling Major Strasser, a sign on the office door tells us that Strasser is working out of the offices of the German Commission of Armistice. **(1:35:11)** And when Strasser buzzes for help, Herr Heinz answers the call.

DID YOU KNOW?: There really was such a commission, though it had a slightly different name—the German Armistice Commission. Launched in connection with Germany's infamous 1940 armistice with France, the commission's main purpose was to ensure that the Vichy French government adhered to its armistice obligations. Regionally, the commission kept a watchful eye on the Vichy French forces.

It seems Herr Heinz enjoyed a rather extravagant tour of duty in Casablanca. In the Casablanca region, the commission had offices just north of the city, in the town of Fedala, and, specifically, in a plush seaside resort called the Miramar Hotel. But had Heinz still been stationed in Casablanca a year later, his good fortune would have come to a sudden end on November 8, 1942. That's when the Allies invaded Morocco and Algeria in a massive amphibious assault code-named Operation Torch.

One of the landing beaches for the operation happened to be right in front of the Miramar Hotel. In the early morning hours, U.S. troops nabbed armistice commission officers on a nearby golf course as they tried to make a mad, pajama-clad dash from the hotel. Hours later, none other than U.S. Major General George Patton had made the Miramar Hotel his springboard headquarters for the planned advance on Casablanca.

All of this means that Heinz could well have been one of the officers captured on the golf course, and Patton and his staff would have been working out of the same offices occupied by Heinz and the visiting Strasser.

RANDOM THOUGHTS: If you want to see the area where Heinz and his fellow commission officers would have hung out during the war, that's easy. The Operation Torch beaches in Fedala (Fedala has since been renamed Mohammedia) are all popular public beaches and easily visited from Casablanca. The massive beach fronting the Miramar Hotel is the one Patton came ashore on.

The Hotel Miramar is no more, but the hotel structures remain on an abandoned and decidedly scruffy lot. A few palm-tree lined paths, once ushering horseback-riding guests out to the beach, hint at the property's former glory. And, somewhat surprisingly, the golf course is still there. It's now part of a prestigious Casablanca-based golf club, and we found it playing tough thanks to brisk ocean breezes.

CLOSER LOOK: Until now, the only direct reference to Hitler in the film was two days ago on the airport tarmac when the welcoming party for Strasser greeted him with a "Heil Hitler" salute. But with just a few minutes left in the film, his likeness appears. Look for Hitler's portrait on the wall as Strasser deduces that something is amiss at the airport. **(1:35:16)**

Casablanca Airport

CLOSER LOOK: The first thing we see at the airport is the plane that will be taking *somebody* to Lisbon in a few moments. **(1:35:24)** Earlier we mentioned that the Lisbon send-off scenes make use of a real plane, and here it is. While these scenes include a mix of real and model planes, this first shot is authentic. The plane is a six-passenger Lockheed 12A Electra Junior, and was built in the late 1930s at Lockheed's Burbank plant, just a few miles away from the Warner Bros. studios. Also visible in this clip is the control tower (with windows illuminated), the fuel truck that Renault and Strasser walked past a few days ago, three men gathered at the plane's door, and two walking around the plane.

FILM ANECDOTES: Sourcing the Electra Junior was no small task for the production team. The main trouble was getting permission from the Army's Fourth Interceptor Command, which was responsible for defending the entire California coast from a Japanese air attack, to fly the desired plane into the Los Angeles Metropolitan Airport for the shoot. Then at the last minute they switched planes to get one with the desired number of windows, presumably to match the model they had already created. Finally, two weeks after the daytime airport scenes were filmed, the second film unit went back out to the airport where they worked until 3:00 a.m. to capture what ended up being a handful of tarmac shots of their preferred plane, totaling less than fifteen seconds. (There are a few other snippets of the

Electra Junior taking off and taxiing that could be authentic as the rendering is spot on for a 12A, but we think the prop team used a model airplane for those shots.)

CLOSER LOOK: The very next shot is from inside the hangar, looking out at the plane on the tarmac. Now, *this* plane is fake, a two-dimensional, quarter-scale rendering of the actual one. It's really not hard to tell the difference but, for what it's worth, the windows are the main tip off. To help create the illusion of a real plane, the production team hired diminutive actors to mill around in front of the mock-up, and then obscured things quite a bit with fake fog. Altogether, not a bad job for a scene filmed entirely on a sound stage.

JUST WONDERING: When the orderly calls in the weather update to the control tower, should he really be reporting visibility at one and one-half miles? We are in a French protectorate, so it should be *kilometers*. Score a gaffe, then, for failing to use the metric system.

RANDOM THOUGHTS: Given the contrived origins of the fog, we were set to point out its use as being inconsistent with actual weather in Casablanca. After all, we're talking about North Africa, where a rather large desert is in the vicinity. But it turns out that fog is not a stranger to Casablanca. Putting on our climatologist's hat for a second, Casablanca's particular location on the Atlantic Ocean subjects it to the classic conditions that produce coastal fog—warm air passing over cold coastline water. That said, fog in Casablanca tends to be a morning (and seasonal) thing.

CLOSER LOOK: A large sign on the wall reading *Défense Absolue de Fumer* makes clear that smoking is strictly prohibited in the hangar. **(1:39:30)** Rick pays no mind. With the sign right in his sight line, Rick lights up a smoke.

EXPLANATION REQUIRED: In the lower right corner of the windshield of Renault's private car is a *roundel*. Roundels are commonly used to mark military aircraft, so we figured it was the Vichy roundel used to designate an official Vichy car. But Vichy used the same roundel as pre-war France—a blue center, a white inner ring and a red outer ring. This one has three rings and a white center. So we're stumped as to whose roundel it is.

CLOSER LOOK: The car Renault drives to the airport is among the film's big-ticket collectibles. It's a 1940 convertible Buick Phaeton; an odd car, we say, to be hanging out in Morocco but certainly an understandable prop compromise. This particular model was quite stylish in its day. The car itself remained in the Warner Bros. film fleet for several decades. Supposedly it appears in another Bogart film, *High Sierra*, though it eluded our eye. Anyway, in 2013 the car exchanged hands at auction for the hefty sum of $461,000.

RANDOM THOUGHTS: Immediately upon Rick, Ilsa, Victor and Renault arriving at the hangar, Rick asks Renault to have his men help Victor find his luggage, prompting Victor to exit stage right. Luggage? What luggage? We didn't see any luggage when Victor arrived at the Café. And wouldn't it be in the car they just arrived in? Where else at the airport could Victor's mystery luggage possibly be? Hey! Stop asking questions. Victor had to be excused, since you can't very well stage one of the most romantic goodbyes in Hollywood history with the woman's husband standing two feet away.

RANDOM THOUGHTS: With the writing now on the wall that Ilsa is going with Victor, not Rick, this is an appropriate time to point out that not once during the film do Victor and Ilsa kiss. And for that matter, they barely touch each other. Instead, all the extra-curricular activity is left for Rick and Ilsa. If this is the extent of the passion between Victor and Ilsa, it looks like this marriage will be coming up short in the romance department.

CLOSER LOOK: Several clips of the Lockheed Electra Junior are mixed in with Victor and Ilsa's last minutes in Casablanca, and they contain some interesting details. In the first two, which show the plane's engines starting, look for the pilot hanging out in the cockpit as well as the logos on the plane's nose.

The circular logo is, of all things, a winged seahorse, and it turns out the logo is authentic to Air France. The airline adopted the logo back in 1933, taking it from one of the four airlines that combined to form Air France. Now, during the daytime airport scene we mentioned that we had spied an Air France flag flying atop the gate to the tarmac. We know that because a winged seahorse logo is barely visible in the flag's center. Running underneath this seahorse logo on the plane's nose, and mostly obscured by it, is a lightning bolt. This was Lockheed's signature paint scheme for the Electra Junior.

In the other two clips, first note the signage by the cabin door, which indicates that in addition to Lisbon and Casablanca the plane also services Tangier, Morocco. **(1:39:54)** Next, note the plane's registration markings, F-AMPJ. Just as the markings on Strasser's plane (D-AGDF) were plausible for one registered in Germany, these markings are plausible for one registered in France. **(1:39:56)** Finally, leaving no doubt that this is meant to be an Air France craft, at the very end of the last shot of the Electra Junior look for the airline's name running above the cabin windows. **(1:40:00)**

So what happened to this particular Electra Junior 12A? Well, accounts have it relocating to the east coast shortly after this shoot, being struck by another plane while taxiing at Mitchel Field in Long Island in October 1942 and written off as irreparable. So yet another plane appearing in *Casablanca* is long gone.

CLOSER LOOK: Strasser is so unnerved by the thought of Victor Laszlo getting out of Casablanca that he foregoes a driver and races to the airport himself. It's an impressive display of self-help for someone of his stature. Like Renault, Strasser is behind the wheel of a Buick convertible, only this one is a 1940 Buick Century. We're guessing this one is not worth quite as much, perhaps in part owing to it being associated with the film's villain.

CLOSER LOOK: So who's a quicker draw, Rick or Strasser? Slow motion reveals that Strasser draws first but Rick gets his shot off just a split second before Strasser. Rick is also a better shot than Strasser. Despite the two achieving near-simultaneous point-blank shots, Strasser somehow misses Rick, while Rick kills Strasser with a single bullet.

DID YOU KNOW?: Early on we alluded to a major difference between the endings for the play and the film. That difference occurs here in the showdown between Rick and Strasser. In the play Rick inexplicably decides not to shoot Strasser and instead gives himself up. Now that definitely does not sound like our Ricky.

CLOSER LOOK: As Strasser falls to the ground like a sack of wheat, watch how he holds onto the phone receiver and in the process breaks off the rather flimsily attached phone cord.

CLOSER LOOK: Let's take a quick look at some background signage. A sign on the hangar's side translates to, Night Service. **(1:41:02)** Inside the hangar are phone numbers for the police, the fire department (*Pompiers*) and the hospital. Quick, someone call for help for poor Strasser! Oh, right, the phone is broken.

Finally, on the wall behind Renault is a French military recruiting poster. In the center is the image of a French colonial soldier. The poster translates to, "Enlist! Reenlist! In the Colonial Army. Ensure Your Future. You Make a Situation." **(1:41:12)** This is actually a typical recruitment poster from the era. You can also find this poster outside the Casablanca courthouse, the Palais de Justice, as the authorities escort the usual suspects inside. **(3:54)**

DID YOU KNOW?: After Strasser is carted away, Renault needs a drink and reaches for a bottle labeled Vichy Water. So was there really such a thing? Most definitely. Apart from hosting France's World War II puppet government, the other thing that Vichy, France is known for is its thermal mineral springs. The springs have been used for therapeutic and medicinal purposes since Roman times. Mineral water connoisseurs consider Vichy water to be vintage stuff; the champagne of mineral waters, you might say.

DID YOU KNOW?: From an authenticity standpoint the bottle's label actually checks out pretty well, with one glaring exception. A French bottle that reads Vichy Water? Though Vichy water had been sold in America since the mid-1800s, we're guessing that bottles with English labels were not making it to a French protectorate in Africa. But we suppose you can't expect American moviegoers to know what Vichy *Eau Minérale* means, so we are giving the prop team a pass here.

As for the rest of the label, in the upper corners are the names of four of Vichy's six mineral springs: Célestins, Grande Grille, Hôpital and Lucas. At the bottom of the label is the full name of an actual French company, Compagnie Fermière de l'établissement thermal de Vichy or CFV. This company had long been running the show in and around the Vichy thermals, including the production and sale of Vichy mineral water, so CFV labeling is a nice touch. Célestins water is what's bottled and sold for recreational drinking. The others are heavier on minerals, including sulfur, and more likely to make you gag than to cure what ails you.

RANDOM THOUGHTS: Of all the beverages referenced in the film—brandy, bourbon, champagne, Champagne Cocktail, Cointreau, coffee, French 75—Vichy water is the one that will not be quaffed. Just as Renault pours himself a glass, he recognizes the water's symbolic meaning, and throws the bottle into the wastebasket.

Interestingly, while we never see Vichy water at Rick's, we happen to know that it's available at the Blue Parrot. Above the bar at Ferarri's establishment is a sign that reads *Eaux Minerales—Vichy Etat.* **(55:28)** *Vichy Etat* and *Etat Français* (*etat* means *state*) were alternative names for the Vichy regime. But, hey, Ferrari is a black market opportunist, not a political ideologue.

DID YOU KNOW?: Having just shot dead an officer of the Third Reich, Rick might want to lay low for a little while. Renault suggests that he head to Brazzaville where there's "a Free French garrison." Today Brazzaville is the capital of the Republic of the Congo. Back in the day it was the capital of French Equatorial Africa, which, we mentioned earlier, Free France wrested away from Vichy in October 1940. For the rest of the war Brazzaville served as the symbolic capital of Free France. Being well off the World War II battle trail, and firmly in Free France hands, Brazzaville would have been an ideal place for Rick and Renault to hole up.

CAST ANECDOTES: Upon returning, in mid-February 1944, from his North Africa and Italy USO tour, Bogart prioritized filming a public service announcement that tied into the tour. In a three-minute short called *Report from the Front*, Bogart urges 1944 movie audiences to donate to the Red Cross. The short provides no details of his trip, but it's well worth viewing for the amusing opening scene.

The cleverly set scene has Bogart at an airport, having just returned from his tour. Bogart and Mayo step off a plane and onto the tarmac. Reporters close in for questions. It's instantly evident that the scene is channeling, full-on, the airport scene in *Casablanca*. And in case anyone in the audience missed the reference, Bogart sports his iconic hat and trench coat ensemble from *Casablanca*. Bogart plays himself, and it's quite funny to see what amounts to Rick Blaine standing in front of a plane to Lisbon, but with Mayo Methot on his arm instead of Ilsa. What follows is Rick, er, Humphrey, looking directly into the camera with quite the compelling pitch, and one that surely inspired 1944 audiences to contribute to the cause.

FILM ANECDOTES: The film's final and now-famous "beautiful friendship" line was by no means a natural. When filming wrapped the first week of August 1942, producer Hal Wallis had not made a decision on the capping line. *Casablanca* could have ended with Rick uttering to Renault one of these uninspired alternatives: "If you ever die a hero's death, heaven protect the angels!" or "I might have known you'd mix your patriotism with a little larceny" or "I begin to see a reason for your sudden attack of patriotism. While you defend your country, you also protect your investment." But in late August, Wallis settled on the "beautiful friendship" line, and called Bogart back in to record it. The final shot— Rick and Renault walking across the tarmac with their backs to the camera—made for an easy dub.

HISTORY LESSON: Filming for *Casablanca* had been a wrap for a mere three months when real-world events suddenly and coincidentally had Americans reading about the war's arrival on the city of Casablanca's front doorstep. Here's the context.

After Germany invaded Russia in June 1941, the Allies considered a second front strategy to, among other things, force Germany to split its military efforts. But the Allies lacked the resources and experience to pull off a near-term direct assault on France, so Allied command embraced an interim plan—take control of North Africa and use it as a base for launching into Europe through Italy.

British troops were already in North Africa, and pushing Axis forces west, back through Libya. The plan, then, was to land additional troops well west of the Axis forces—specifically, in Morocco and Algeria—thereby enabling the Allies to converge on Axis forces from the east and west and corner them in Tunisia. So on November 8, 1942, the Allies launched the aforementioned amphibious invasion of Morocco and Algeria, code-named Operation Torch.

In Morocco, one of the operation's mission-critical objectives was the immediate capture of Casablanca. So how did it go? Well, taking Casablanca should have been easy. The Vichy French coastal defense was not formidable, while the Allies dedicated a one-hundred-plus ship armada, sailing direct from Virginia with some 35,000 U.S. troops, to three main landing areas in Morocco. What's more, two U.S. military heavyweights were in charge of carrying out the Casablanca-area maneuvers: General Patton and Rear Admiral Henry Hewitt.

The main landing area dedicated to capturing Casablanca was northeast of the city, at the town of Fedala, and things went anything but smoothly there. The task force struggled mightily just to get ashore. Dozens of landing craft overturned in the rocks and challenging surf, spilling soldiers and essential equipment into the ocean. Drowning casualties were shockingly high. Landed supplies were so minimal that Patton could not immediately advance toward Casablanca despite it being just fifteen miles down the coast. Patton later conceded that if enemy resistance had been greater, the task force would have been in a spot.

And while land-based enemy fire was light, the Vichy French navy had more than a few ships parked in Casablanca's harbor—which is right downtown—and quickly engaged the Allies in a full-on sea battle. Fierce shelling exchanges ensued in and around the harbor; numerous ships on both sides were hobbled or sunk. Allied fighters raced above the harbor, strafing ships and key structures.

As the Allies slowly took control of the air and sea around Casablanca, Allied troops finally began flowing down from Fedala. By the end of Day Three, Allied ground forces, converging from Fedala and another main landing area south of Casablanca, had the city surrounded.

Finally, in the early hours of November 11, Vichy French commanders relayed to Patton a message of surrender. And it's a good thing because Patton, despite having no military orders to do so, was set to move forward that morning with a full-blown attack on Casablanca, and there's little doubt he would have leveled it.

RANDOM THOUGHTS: By the way, while Casablanca's harbor has expanded over the decades, it still includes much of the footprint that existed in 1942. That means you can easily pinpoint where key battle events occurred, such as the spot where the Vichy French battleship *Jean Bart* was parked when the U.S. Navy took it out.

JUST WONDERING: So what would Operation Torch have meant for our *Casablanca* characters? Well Ferrari, Carl and anyone else who stuck around certainly would have been in the thick of things when Operation Torch hit Casablanca's shores. We know that Rick's Café is right next to the airport, which means anyone daring enough could have sat on the café's terrace—right where Rick and Renault chatted on the first night—and watched the Allies swarm and capture the airport and transform it into a Allied military air base. And the Blue Parrot is in the medina, which is just a stone's throw from the harbor, where the heaviest bombing took place. So we're guessing both establishments would have been shuttered for a week or so, but not long thereafter business would have soared as Allied personnel poured into Casablanca and the city became the Allies' main personnel entry point and supply hub for the North Africa Theater.

CAST ANECDOTES: Bogart's North Africa wartime travels included a visit with U.S. troops at an air base in Port Lyautey, a few hours north of Casablanca, which the Allies captured from the Vichy French during Operation Torch in an intense battle. There, Bogart lost more than a few dollars playing craps with the boys. We say, he should have stuck to playing chess.

FILM ANECDOTES: Operation Torch nearly changed the ending of *Casablanca*. As the invasion unfolded in and around Casablanca, producer Hal

Wallis apparently decided that the ending needed to dovetail with current events. Just three days after the invasion, he fired off a memorandum ordering a retake of the final scene. The revised ending was to take place at night on the fog-blanketed deck of a Free France freighter, with interior shots set in the ship's radio room. Rick and Renault were to be accompanied by several dozen uniformed Free France crewmen, presumably whisking the two away from Casablanca to a Free France holding. But, with some time to reflect, Wallis called off the involved retake, in part because Rains had already returned to his home in Pennsylvania.

FILM ANECDOTES: The film's November 26, 1942, premiere in New York, was designed to piggyback on the steady stream of news surrounding Operation Torch and the capture of Casablanca. But that was just a limited release; the national release did not occur until January 23, 1943. Well, January would bring with it another war-related topical boost for the film. Just a day after the national release, Roosevelt and Churchill shocked the world by announcing they had just wrapped up secret war room meetings in, of all places, the city of Casablanca.

HISTORY LESSON: The Casablanca Conference, as it became known, took place in Casablanca's upscale Anfa neighborhood, just a few miles down the coast from the city's downtown harbor. The Allies essentially transformed a bucolic Anfa hilltop into a comfortable, high-security military compound. Here are some insider conference specifics:

- The conference compound centered on a large hilltop roundabout. The Hotel Anfa, which served as the conference hub, sat in the middle of the roundabout. Roosevelt and Churchill stayed in villas located on the outer edge of the roundabout; Patton stayed in a villa down the hill a ways.

- While the Hotel Anfa is long gone, Roosevelt and Churchill's villas are still standing. Churchill's villa is now the residence of the U.S. Consul General in Casablanca.

- Because of Roosevelt's restricted mobility, many strategy sessions and casual gatherings took place at his villa. With its elegant art deco features, the villa flows breezily from its entrance to the back terrace, making life easier on the wheelchair-bound Roosevelt. On the first floor is a bedroom where Roosevelt slept, a high-ceilinged living room where Roosevelt huddled with top advisors and shared drinks with Churchill, and a dining room where Roosevelt and Churchill dined with the Sultan of Morocco.

- The truly historic space in Roosevelt's villa is in the back garden, and, save the updated garden pool, the visuals have scarcely changed over the decades. There, on a patch of grass just a few feet off the back corner of the trellis-covered terrace, Roosevelt and Churchill disclosed their secret war conference to a mesmerized press corps, and then famously declared to the world that the Allies would accept nothing less than the enemy's unconditional surrender. It was, to borrow Rick's phrasing, the moment when destiny seemed to take a hand for the Allies...and for Good.

FILM ANECDOTES: With the city of Casablanca now tied to feel-good wartime events, it's easy to understand why American moviegoers would want to head out the door and see the film by the same name. And those who did were treated to the ultimate winner of the Academy Award for Best Picture of 1943.

Due to the war, the Academy Awards ceremony for 1943 (held in March 1944) was a low-key, no-frills affair. That meant a theater setting instead of a dinner-and-drinks banquet, painted plaster statuettes instead of metal ones in sensitivity to wartime metal shortages, and a tight schedule to make the live radio broadcast more listener-friendly for troops overseas.

Casablanca entered the night with eight nominations and came away with three winners—Best Picture, Best Director and Best Adapted Screenplay—second to *The Song of Bernadette's* four. While *Casablanca's* three wins were impressive, it could easily have been more. No one would have blinked if, say, Bogart and Rains had won their respective nominations for Best Actor and Best Supporting Actor.

CAST ANECDOTES: Ingrid Bergman was also in the mix that night for an Oscar, but not for *Casablanca*. Instead, she was a Best Actress nominee for her performance in *For Whom the Bell Tolls*, which outpaced Casablanca at the box office despite a much later release date. This was Bergman's first of seven Academy Award nominations. Jennifer Jones took home the statuette, but Bergman's star was so bright that many saw her time coming and soon. And sure enough, the very next year she won her first of three Academy Awards—Best Actress in *Gaslight*. Add in her 1945 Best Actress nomination for *The Bells of St. Mary's*, and she and her films had quite an impressive three-year showing at the Academy Awards.

FILM ANECDOTES: One famously awkward moment at the Academy Awards that year came when *Casablanca's* name was called for Best Picture. Having been at the helm for *Casablanca's* production, Hal Wallis fully expected to accept the award. But studio head Jack Warner had other ideas. When

Casablanca won, Warner darted to the stage "with the speed of antelope," as described by gossip columnist Hedda Hopper. Meanwhile, Wallis, having failed to anticipate the strategic value of an aisle seat, got pinned in his row and was left watching from his seat in stunned disbelief.

Whoa! Talk about your plot twists. Well, these days it's clear that the Best Picture award goes to producers, but back then it was still a little fuzzy. Studio heads had been known to accept from time to time. And further clouding things, Jack Warner is named as the film's executive producer in the opening credits.

We say, while Wallis may have had a legitimate claim to being on stage, he misplayed the situation. He knew his relationship with Warner was at an all-time low, and he also knew that Warner was, at heart, a self-promoter. So, really, Wallis should have seen it coming and set Warner straight before the ceremony, or, at the very least, brokered their mutual appearance onstage.

JUST WONDERING: So was there any noticeable drama when Warner hit the stage to the exclusion of Wallis? We tracked down the ceremony's radio broadcast, and while there are no gasps or rumblings from the audience, the show's host, comedian Jack Benny, sure had a strange reaction. Twice he asked who was going to accept the award. Benny then seemed to feign surprise at Warner's sudden appearance onstage. It was as if Benny sensed that an injustice was unfolding and was trying to buy time for someone to shout Wallis' name or for Wallis to come forward. Neither happened, and after a few Benny wisecracks at Warner's expense, Warner pressed on, solo.

FILM ANECDOTES: Warner's Best Picture acceptance speech was all of forty seconds and unremarkable. To his credit he did thank Wallis first, albeit without elaboration. He went on to thank, in order, Curtiz, Bogart, Bergman, Greenstreet and Lorre. Poor Claude Rains and Paul Henreid—at least Wallis didn't have to suffer through the indignity of not being mentioned at all. Warner then defaulted to thanking "the rest of the cast," while confessing he had not prepared because he didn't think *Casablanca* would win. Hmmm. That must have further frosted Wallis, who surely had a pithy *Casablanca* acceptance speech at the ready.

FILM ANECDOTES: Unfortunately for Wallis, the awkwardness of the moment did not end with Warner bounding off the stage, Oscar in hand. The very next award was the Irving G. Thalberg Memorial Award, which is a special non-Oscar award for consistently outstanding work by a producer on films produced during the year. Wallis had won the Thalberg once before for his work in 1938, and wouldn't you know it, he won it again. So just minutes after being left out of the Best Picture acceptance, Wallis found himself stepping into the spotlight to accept an award that was largely in recognition of his production of *Casablanca*. The Thalberg award is no doubt prestigious, but in the moment it must have felt a bit like winning Miss Congeniality at the beauty pageant. In an emotionless ten-second speech, Wallis thanked no one specifically.

FILM ANECDOTES: For Wallis, the night's episode was his sign that he needed to leave Warner Bros. His increasingly prickly relationship with Jack Warner seemed unsalvageable. He should have been riding high from his objectively stellar showing at the Academy Awards. Instead, he focused on how to exit the studio. Just days after the ceremony, newspapers began reporting that Wallis was exploring options and a break up was coming. Soon thereafter, Warner Bros. reassigned Wallis' films. By the end of May he was gone, re-launching as an independent producer with Paramount ties.

FILM ANECDOTES: Just a few days after the ceremony, Hedda Hopper provided some perspective on the Wallis-Warner incident, writing in her column: "This fighting for personal glory seems so silly. The public doesn't give a hoot who produced what or when. All they're interested in is: Is it a good picture?" Indeed, history didn't care who accepted the award. There was plenty of credit to spread around for *Casablanca's* success, and Wallis and Warner were forever connected to a film for the ages.

FILM MUSIC

Casablanca has a blockbuster lineup of popular songs. Some songs were picked to fit the moment, but many made the cut simply because they were owned by Warner Bros.

"It Had To Be You" (Kahn-Jones)—first song sung by Sam at the Café.

"Shine" (Brown-Dabney-Mack)—sung by Sam at the Café.

"Knock On Wood" (Jerome-Scholl)—sung by Sam at the Café.

"The Very Thought Of You" (Ray Noble)—piano instrumental played twice at the Café, on the first night as Ferrari and Rick discuss Sam's future, and again on the second night as Sascha and Carl thank Rick for helping the Bulgarian couple win at roulette.

"Baby Face" (Davis-Akst)—sung by Sam at the Café.

"I'm Just Wild About Harry" (Sissle-Blake)—piano instrumental playing when Renault and his men prepare for Ugarte's arrest.

"Heaven Can Wait" (DeLange-Van Heusen)—piano instrumental played by Sam after Rick apologizes to his patrons for the disturbance caused by Ugarte's arrest.

"Speak To Me Of Love" (Jean Lenoir)—piano instrumental playing when Victor and Ilsa enter the Café for the first time.

"Love For Sale" (Cole Porter)—piano instrumental played at the Café when Renault interrupts Victor and Ilsa's meeting with fellow Resistance member Berger.

"Tango Delle Rose" (Schreier-Bottero)—played and sung by Señorita Andreya at the Café.

"Avalon" (Jolson-Rose)—piano instrumental played by Sam just before he plays "As Time Goes By" for Ilsa.

"As Time Goes By" (Herman Hupfeld)—played and sung by Sam for Ilsa at the Café and in La Belle Aurore during the Paris flashback. Melodic quotations from song also used throughout the film.

"Perfidia" (Dominguez-Leeds)—played as Rick and Ilsa slow dance in a nightclub during the Paris flashback.

"If I Could Be With You (One Hour Tonight)" (Creamer-Johnson)—played at the Café on the second night as the pickpocket performs his craft at the bar and as Rick and Renault share a drink.

"You Must Have Been A Beautiful Baby" (Mercer-Warren)—played at the Café on the second night as Yvonne enters the Café.

"Die Wacht am Rhein" (Schneckenburger-Wilhelm)—played during the second night at the Café.

"La Marseillaise" (Rouget de Lisle)—played during the second night at the Café. Short quotations from song also used throughout the film.

"Das Lied der Deutschen" (Haydn-Hoffmann von Fallersleben)—short melodic quotations used throughout the film, including the Paris flashback, the second night at the Café and the airport scene at film's end.

Michael Willian is a writer, film buff and corporate executive and attorney. He is the author of a film guidebook for another American classic, *It's a Wonderful Life*, titled *The Essential It's a Wonderful Life: A Scene-by-Scene Guide to the Classic Film.* Michael grew up in the Chicago area and calls Chicago home.

Printed in France by Amazon
Brétigny-sur-Orge, FR